BOYS TOWN
Prayer
Book

Father Val J. Peter, Editor

Boys Town, Nebraska

Boys Town Prayer Book

Copyright © 2002 by Father Flanagan's Boys' Home

Published by The Boys Town Press
14100 Crawford St.
Boys Town, NE 68010
boystownpress.org
1-800-282-6657

Boys Town Press is the publishing division of Boys Town, a national organization serving children and families.

10 9 8 7 6 5 4

"Every boy must learn to pray, how he prays is up to him."

— Father Edward J. Flanagan
1927

Table of Contents

Introduction

Prayers for Special Times and Needs

Reflections and Prayers
By Boys Town Youth

Father Flanagan Speaks to Youth

Traditional Catholic Prayers

Traditional Protestant Prayers

Youth Psalms

Hymn-Poems to Pray
in the Quiet of One's Room

A Final Word

Dear Children of Boys Town,

Father Edward J. Flanagan, the founder of Boys Town, was a person of great prayer. He prayed every day and insisted that "his boys" should learn to pray well too.

What did he think about the importance of prayer?

"Pray, for prayer can work miracles. The child in an unreligious home hasn't got a chance."

"Without God at the beginning, there can only be confusion at the end."

"The whole family should unite in a community prayer each night to bring back God to the home and rebuild it as a spiritual unit of a hoped-for new world."

This is a book I hope you will use very often. I hope you will pray especially at times when you feel down or lonely. It contains many prayers. It contains both traditional prayers and prayers written by Boys Town children who have gone before you and who have had experiences and feelings very much like your own.

If you learn nothing else at Boys Town, I hope you learn that your prayer invites God to come intimately into your life, changing you and changing the circumstances in which you live – for the better. I pray for each of you every day. Please pray for me too and for all of us who love you and cherish you, now and always.

Sincerely yours,

Fr. Val J. Peter, JCD, STD
Executive Director Emeritus

P.S. I hope others, especially children, use our *Boys Town Prayer Book* as well. It can be a source of great help and hope for you also.

The Boys Town Creed

Boys Town: All our endeavors are founded on the conviction that the hope of the future lies in the wholesome development of the youth of today. Boys Town is dedicated to helping all boys and girls realize their full potential for God, self and society.

We believe in a Supreme Being, our Creator and loving Father.

We believe in the sanctity of human life from its conception to its entrance into eternal life.

We believe that every youth should pray; how he or she prays is a matter of personal choice.

We believe in helping youth of any creed or ethnic background and in developing the total person: the physical, mental and spiritual.

We believe in helping physically handicapped as well as socially deprived youth and in respecting the human rights of each individual.

We believe in the pursuit of truth within a framework of religious principles.

We believe that our Boys Town motto, "He ain't heavy, Father...he's m' brother," characterizes our concern for every youth, whatever his or her burden.

The Boys Town Prayer

You may not realize it, but you are a very fortunate young person. Why? Because thousands of people all over the United States are praying for YOU each day. And that means God is sending a lot of grace your way. This is the prayer thousands of our friends and donors say each day for you and all the boys and girls here. Perhaps you would like to say it, too, for yourself and your friends.

Dear Lord,

Help every child at Boys Town this day. Make each of them feel loved and wanted and cared for and appreciated. When they are down, give them a lift. When they are hurt, give them healing. When they cry, dry their tears. When they run away, bring them safely home. When they fall, pick them up and hold them ever close to Your heart in the palm of Your hand. Finally, Lord, fill their lives with faith, hope and love now and forever. Amen.

Father Flanagan's Sayings

Read these wise words from Father Flanagan, our founder, and let their meaning sink into your hearts and minds.

"No motive for good lives can exceed religion in its power. God and God alone in the lives of fathers and mothers, boys and girls, can best teach the laws of right and social living. The well being of society and of the individuals who compose it, depends on their observance."

"There is wisdom in the habit of looking at the bright side of life."

"Our young people are our greatest wealth. Give them a chance and they will give a good account of themselves."

"Pray, for prayer can work miracles. The child in an unreligious home hasn't got a chance."

"There are no bad boys. There is only bad environment, bad training, bad example, bad thinking."

"As long as a people or nation puts its trust in God, that people or nation will always be happy. That nation is rich in depth, width and height of strong character and strong citizenship."

"You have learned, during your stay here, the proper principles on which a real and successful life is founded. You have built characters on love and service. As long as you keep before your mind these great and eternal truths – you shall not fail."

"Often, it has been said that youth is the nation's greatest asset. But it is more than that – it is the world's greatest asset. More than that, it is perhaps, the world's only hope."

"A true religious training for children is most essential if we are to expect to develop them into good men and good women – worthy citizens of our great country."

"I feel that all growth must come from inside – by starting with yourself you boys should realize that within you, you have the germ of goodness, based upon faith in Almighty God."

Prayer Is...

A is for Adoration.
> This means to give praise to God: "I adore."

C is for Confession.
> This means to confess to God: "I confess."

T is for Thanksgiving.
> This means to thank God: "I am thankful."

S is for Supplication.
> This means to ask God: "I ask."

A Sample Prayer:

> **A** – O God, I praise you for the gift of my life.
>
> **C** – I confess that I do not always act according to your Law of Love.
>
> **T** – I thank you for the many gifts you give me each day.
>
> **S** – I ask that you protect my friends and family. In Jesus' name I pray. Amen.

Prayers for Special Times and Needs

Detail from Window in Dowd Memorial Chapel,
Boys Town Campus

Morning Prayer

Dear Lord,

You have made another beautiful day. You have given this day to me as a gift to enjoy. Thank You for the sun and the clouds, the wind and the rain. It is Your gift to me and I thank You. I will enjoy Your gift this day, dear Lord, especially the little things: the smell of breakfast, the song in my heart, the sight of Your flowers, the touch of Your hand, and knowing all this beauty is Your gift to me. I promise You, Lord, I will not hurt myself today with sad thoughts from my past or bitter memories of disappointment. You have given me a beautiful day and I will receive it with joy and gladness. Amen.

Evening Prayer

Thank You, Lord, for a beautiful day. Your good earth has this day surrounded me with faith. Your sky has this day inspired me with hope. My brothers and sisters have this day shared with me their love. Thank you for the good food and those I shared it with. Thank You for my happy thoughts. Thank You for my kindly deeds. Thank You for people. Thank You for their caring. Thank You for their sharing. Thank You for not letting me hurt myself today with sad thoughts or bitter memories. I'm glad You created me. I'm glad You created this day. Good night, dear Lord. Amen.

Another Night Prayer

O God, before I sleep, I remember before You all the people I love, and now in the silence, I say their names to You. All the people who are sad and lonely, old and forgotten, poor and hungry and cold, in pain of body and in distress of mind. Bless all who specially need Your blessing, and bless me too, and make this a good night for me. This I ask for Your love's sake.

— WILLIAM BARCLAY

In Time of Discouragement

Dear Lord,

My troubles seem to hem me in on every side. I am so very discouraged. I even wonder if there is any meaning or purpose in my many troubles. Lord, please help me to open my eyes to the good things of my life. Let me see the beauty in my relationship with You, dear Lord. Even if no one else were to care for me, You will be there at my side to love me and to give me hope. I can count on You in the darkness of the night and in the midst of the storm. Let me remember that the most frequently repeated words of Yours to use in the gospels are: "Do not be afraid, I am with You." Be with me now. I am opening the door of my heart. Come and dwell with me. Amen.

Prayer for the Deceased

Dear Lord,

Please give eternal rest to my loved ones. The fever of life is over for them. I miss them so very much. They brought me so much joy and hope. Let me remember, dear Lord, that I brought them also happiness and love. Let me remember the daily bread we ate together, sometimes in joy on birthdays and holidays, and sometimes in sadness at funerals and times of tragedy.

Let me remember the future, that with faith and trust in God and our sins forgiven, we will meet each other again in heaven and enjoy all eternity together. Have mercy on them, O Lord. Grant them eternal rest and give me the courage and strength and peace I need in these difficult days. Amen.

For Healing

Dear Lord,

I have been very hard on myself. I make demands on myself which are too harsh. I judge myself too severely. I have put myself down too often. That is how l grew up. That is how I was taught. Dear Lord, I am putting myself in Your presence. I am one with You, God, as well as with others. I am not going to hurt myself or others anymore. I am now experi-

encing being cared for and guided by You, God.
Dear Lord, please heal my soul, mind, and body
and that of all people now. I rest in Your peace and
healing today and forever. Amen.

Prayer Before Meals

Give us, Lord, a bit of sun,
    a bit of talk and a bit of fun.

Give us in all our laughter and sputter,
    our daily bread and a bit of butter.

Give us health our keep to make,
    and a bit to spare for the others' sake.

Give us too a life of song,
    and a tale and a book to help us along.

Give us, Lord, a chance to be,
    our goodly best, brave, wise and free.

Our goodly best for ourselves and others,
    'til all of us learn to live as brothers.

We ask this in your name, Amen.

In Time of Sickness

Dear Lord,

I feel hemmed in on all sides by my sickness. The pain is bad enough. But the fear and anxiety are a greater affliction. Hear, O Lord, the sound of my weeping and my cry for help. Hear, O Lord, and have pity for me. I offer You my sorrows and sickness. Let them be my prayer to You. I offer up this pain for troubled and abandoned children everywhere. Heal them. Heal me too. And give me courage and strength and hope in abundance. Amen.

Prayer for a Family

Dear Lord,

You have put in our hearts a love for family. Thank You for the beauty in our family. Let us be kind, even when others are not kind to us. Let us be patient, even when others are impatient. Let us be peace makers, even when others want to fight. Let us cool our anger down when we are upset. Let us be the first to ask forgiveness when others refuse to do so. Help us to praise and encourage each other this day. Amen.

For Forgiveness

Dear God,

Please help me now to forgive myself and others all our mistakes. Thank You for all the blessings You have given me in my life. Please heal my soul, mind, and body and that of all people now. I am God's beloved child. You, God, love me very much. I am one with God and myself, even if my troubles with others are many.

Thank You, Lord, for coming into my heart this moment. Please make Your home in my heart. Please let me enjoy this peace now. It is beautiful to have You with me. Amen.

— JUDITH NIMBI

Prayer for Children

Dear Lord,

While on earth, Your anger glowed mightily against the harm done by those who hurt or scandalized children through carelessness, cruelty, and lust. Bring all adults to see their failures which increase the unhappiness of children. Lord, we hereby promise to bring the aid people need that will keep them from hurting our children again and again. Lord have mercy on us. Increase our determination to help by word, deed, and prayer all children facing dangers of body, mind and spirit. Help all children who are hungry or homeless. Bind up the wounds of children of broken homes. Care for frightened and lonely children who look for love and do not find it. Dear Lord, have mercy on our children in their suffering. Have mercy on us in our sins. Bring us the determination to open our hearts to Your grace so our lives may be changed and our children's lives may be healed. Amen.

Prayer for a Parent

O God, Creator and Redeemer of all the faithful, look down with gracious eyes on us, fathers and mothers of this world. Teach us to know and understand the high position which we as parents hold in Thy Divine plan of creation – the guardianship of Thy precious little ones.

Give us, dear Lord, the strength and patience to teach by example and precept our precious children and lead them along the paths of virtue, onward and upward toward Thee, their loving and all gracious God. All this we ask in Thy name. Amen.

– FATHER EDWARD J. FLANAGAN

Lord, You Too Were Once a Student

Lord, You too were once a student just like me. You studied God's word, and You learned the history of Your people, and You were taught a trade and household chores as well. You grew up in a family and advanced in wisdom and age and grace.

Dear Lord, help me always to open my mind to seek the truth of things. Help me to be a good student. Help me to desire to learn as much as I can. And give me hope and strength to live my life and follow in Your footsteps. In Your name we pray. Amen.

A Student's Prayer

Sometimes it is very hard to be a student. Some days I don't want to go to school. It is very hard to learn. I failed in school too often in the past, and I sometimes don't trust my teachers.

Dear Lord, please help me study when I would rather watch television. Please encourage me when I want to give up. Please help me to sit down and study. Please give me a greater desire to learn and to know.

Sometimes Lord, I don't give myself credit enough. I can learn things better than I think. I know that with Your help and love, I really can succeed in school. Help me, too, to encourage my fellow students and say a word of praise to them when they do well. I know You love me, Lord. Help me to love Your truth and goodness and beauty. Amen.

The Road Ahead

My Lord God,
I have no idea where I am going. I do not see the road ahead of me. I cannot know for certain where it will end. Nor do I really know myself, and the fact that I think that I am following Your will does not mean that I am actually doing so.

But I believe that the desire to please You does, in fact, please You. And I hope I have that desire in all that I am doing. I hope that I will never do anything apart from that desire. I know that if I do this, You will lead me by the right road, though I may know nothing about it.

Therefore, will I trust You always, though I may seem to be lost and in the shadow of death. I will not fear, for You are ever with me, and You will not leave me to face my perils alone. Amen.

– Thomas Merton

Prayer for My Roommate

Why in heaven's name, Lord did You give me this roommate rather than someone else? I really don't know the answer. I do trust You, Lord, that You have sent this roommate so that I might learn something and grow in some important way. Help me to be patient and kind and understanding, even if I do not receive patience and kindness in return. Give me the courage I need and the strength to do Your will. To learn to grow in appreciation of other human beings, including my roommate. Thank You, Lord, for Your blessings. Amen.

For Good Attitudes Toward Sex

Lord, sometimes I get very, very confused about sex. I have a deep drive or need within me which I can feel and sometimes I think it is going to drive me crazy. Then when I go and act out these drives, I really am bothered by what I have done and I feel pretty terrible about myself.

Dear Lord, help me to express myself appropriately. Help me to show affection without degrading myself or anyone else. Help me not to be afraid to show affection appropriately, and help me to say no when I really should and want to say no. Help me, especially, not be intimidated, bullied or manipulated into doing things I really don't want to do. Help me not to be afraid and not to be ashamed.

Help me to realize that You have given me the gift of my sexuality. Help me not to be afraid to say I am sorry to You, Lord, as I know You will forgive me. Help me to accept myself in joy and gratitude. Amen.

For Our Parents in Trouble

Dear Lord,

I ask You to give Your help to those of us who have parents in trouble. So often parents are angry at each other. Lord, give mom and dad courage to take away the bitterness in their hearts. Dear Lord, when parents are out of work, help them find a new job. When troubles of sickness and alcoholism and drugs might sap their strength, bind up their wounds and mend the brokenness of their lives.

Dear Lord, You have given me these parents. Help them not to be abusive to themselves or to me or to each other. Help us to learn better to live in peace and harmony. And help me to forgive and heal the harm and wrongs that have been done to me, without allowing them to happen again. Thank You, Lord, for Your help now and always. Amen.

Reflections and Prayers by Our Boys Town Youth

Two Boys Town residents, 1921

When You're Feeling Homesick

Lord, in my times of homesickness, I prayed and You comforted me. When things weren't going my way, I wanted to escape, to run away from it all. Instead, You intervened. You consoled me and helped me get over my troubles. Thank You, Lord.

— SAM

That prayer was written by a Boys Town youth who felt just like you do. Here's what other boys and girls have done to help themselves when they felt homesick.

When I first got here, I was really lonely. I didn't want to do anything the other guys did and I always stayed in my room. Then I decided before I came here, I was never home anyway. I was running around all night and getting into trouble. So I decided Boys Town was the place for me.

— DEREK

Being homesick is nothing to be ashamed of. It just means you have been away from your family longer than usual. We all have homesickness some time in our life.

When I get homesick, I just sit and think about all the good I am getting from this place that I couldn't get at home. If I went home, I would probably pick up my old bad habits again. I remember that I wanted to find some place new and better, and I found it.

— MICHELLE

Whenever I get homesick I remember all the trouble I was into before I came to Boys Town. I think about how much better I am doing at school here than at home. I keep busy by singing in the choir, playing in the band, playing football and wrestling. These all make me feel good about myself.

— DOUG

When I feel homesick, I talk with the other guys in my house. I do things to take my mind off home, like playing football or basketball.

— JOSE

Try to make new friends and close relationships with the people around you. That is what I have done. Homesickness will happen to you all of your life whenever you go someplace new. You need to learn to cope with it now. Above all, be sure to talk with your Family-Teachers when you feel home-sick. That really helps me.

— TAMMY

You must have had the experience of walking
  along the edge of the sea,
Or a lake on a summer's evening when the
  moonlight shimmered across the waves.
Whether or not you noticed, the beam of light
  reflecting off the water
Shone directly at your feet.
It always does, no matter if there are a million
  people walking along the shore, each individual,
  when he stops and looks up,
  sees a shaft of light
Shining at his feet. There is something in the
  nature of light
Which makes it so, just as there is something in
  the nature of God's being that reaches out to us
  – individually.
When we stop and look up, the light of His love is
  radiantly directed at each of us and the dark
  patch ahead
Is no longer dark...

– JASON

When you are feeling homesick, pray the following:

"The Lord is my shepherd, I shall lack nothing. He
makes me lie down in green pastures, He leads me
beside quiet waters, He restores my soul. He guides
me in paths of righteousness for His name's sake.

Even though I walk through the valley of the shadow of death, I will fear no evil, for You are with me; Your rod and Your staff, they comfort me.

"You prepare a table before me in the presence of my enemies. You anoint my head with oil; my cup overflows. Surely goodness and love will follow me all the days of my life, and I will dwell in the house of the Lord forever."

– PSALM 23

When You Want to Run Away

I packed my bag and got it ready to go.
I did it quietly, so no one would know.
I crept through the house, that was dark as night;
I wanted to leave, 'cause nothin' was going right.
I opened the door through which I would split.
My mind acted heavy and I had to think about it.
If I took off and never came back,
In the mid of my life, there'd be a major crack.
I went to my room and laid on the bed.
And asked God to help me clear my head.
God helped me out and showed me the way.
And that's the reason I'm here today.
If you feel like taking off and wanting to quit,
Let God help you out and pray about it.

– MARTY

Whether you're new at Boys Town or have been here for a time, you may have thought that running away would be easier than staying. But, as the boy who wrote the above poem did, you might have second thoughts. Here's what some others have done.

The power I had to resist from running away didn't come from my mind, but from my heart and from God. I had to discipline myself to not choose what I wanted, but what was right. Whenever you are faced with a problem, look at it in perspective. Say to yourself, "What can I do to make the situation better?" Remember, if you do the right things, the situation can only improve. When you are in trouble, ask God to pull you through.

– MIKE

Whenever I wanted to run away, I would sit and think about all the things that could happen to me while I was gone. I thought about my placement here and how much I would lose by running and how little I would gain. Then I would talk to my Family-Teachers if I still had the urge to run away. Sometimes they would help a lot, and other times they would let me have my privacy and space to myself for a while. It works.

– KERRY

I sometimes thought of running away when times weren't the best, but then I looked at my situation in perspective. I thought to myself, "If I were to run away, everyone would worry about me and wonder if I was okay." Also, it wouldn't help matters any, it would just make them worse. Always look ahead. There is no use in dealing with the past, there is no future in it. So, when you are down and thinking of running, ask someone to help you through it. I did that several times and didn't regret it.

— KAREEM

When you leave, you are hurting no one but yourself. You only set yourself up to get sent some place really bad. At the time, you think this is the worst place on earth. But if you think about it, there are millions of other kids in the world who would give anything to sleep in your warm bed. Boys Town is a blessing.

— TONY

When things started going bad for me and everyone was on my case about something and I couldn't stay out of trouble, I used to think about running away and starting over. Then I would stop and think: What would happen to my education if I left? What if I got caught — where would they put me? What if I got hurt or killed? Running away could be the solution to one problem, but it could create many more.

— ANNA

***When you feel like running away, remember what
Our Lord says:***

"Come to me, all you who labor and are heavy bur-
dened and I will give you rest. Take my yoke upon
you and learn of me. For I am meek and humble of
heart. And you will find rest for your souls. For my
yoke is easy and my burden light."

– MATTHEW 11:28-30

***And what St. Paul says in his letter to the
Philippians:***

"Rejoice in the Lord always. I will say it again:
Rejoice! Let your gentleness be evident to all. The
Lord is near. Do not be anxious about
anything, but in everything, by prayer and
petition, with thanksgiving, present your requests
to God. And the peace of God, which transcends all
understanding, will guard your hearts and your
minds in Christ Jesus.

"Finally, brothers, whatever is true, whatever is
noble, whatever is right, whatever is pure,
whatever is lovely, whatever is admirable – if anything is excellent or praiseworthy – think about
such things."

When You're Tempted
to Use Drugs or Alcohol

God, grant me serenity to accept the things I cannot change, the courage to change the things I can, and the wisdom to know the difference. Amen.

This prayer, says a Boys Town youth, helps him get through the urge to do drugs and alcohol. Many of you have been and will be tempted to turn to drugs to solve problems or just to "have fun." Here are some things to do when tempted to use drugs.

I talk to the Lord when I think about taking drugs to ease depression. There's not a problem that God can't fix. Drugs only create problems and hold you back from the hopes and dreams and goals you've planned.

— JAKE

When I am tempted to do drugs, I first of all say: "No. I will never touch another chemical substance no matter what." They ruin you physically and mentally. I told my friend he was wrong to offer me drugs when he knew I was trying to kick the habit.

— CHRISTINE

I can think of a million times when I've been tempted by drugs. Sometimes I just said no and turned
away from them. Other times the temptations were
so great that I couldn't just turn away. Instead, I
failed and said "Why not?" Every time I said, "No,"
I felt very good about myself. But every time I said,
"Why not?" I felt very guilty and down.

– Scott

Before I came here, I was heavily into drugs. When
I got here, I didn't care about anything or anybody.
Now that I have started praying, it has brought me
closer to God. I became afraid for my friends back
home who were still doing drugs. So I started to
pray for them and a lot of them have changed for
the better.

– Lindsay

I used to use drugs extensively. It got to the point
where the first thing I thought about in the morning was how to get some pot. I ended up in a pit, a
helpless pit. Finally, I got sent to a drug treatment
facility. I found out I don't need drugs, that I am an
okay person.

They introduced me to God. They taught me to pray
to Him for help. And I did. I prayed constantly and
soon all my pressure was gone.

– Stacy

I talk to God to take away the urge to do drugs. Drugs might help me relax and hide from the world for a while, but since I've been here I can talk to God and He helps me to overcome the urge. I want to make my mother proud of me and go on to better things.

– TODD

When you're tempted to take drugs, read these Scripture passages:

"Blessed is the person who does not walk in the counsel of the wicked or stand in the way of sinners or sit in the seat of mockers. But his delight is in the law of the Lord, and on His law he meditates day and night. He is like a tree planted by streams of water, which yields its fruit in season and whose leaf does not wither. Whatever he does he prospers.

"Not so the wicked. They are like chaff that the wind blows away. Therefore, the wicked will not stand in the judgment, nor sinners in the assembly of the righteous.

"For the Lord watches over the way of the righteous, but the way of the wicked will perish."

– PSALM 1

"Watch and pray so that you will not fall into temptation. The spirit is willing, but the body is weak."

– MATTHEW 26:41

"So, if you think you are standing firm, be careful that you don't fall! No temptation has seized you except what is common to us. And God is faithful; He will not let you be tempted beyond what you can bear. But when you are tempted, He will also provide a way out so that you can stand up under it."

– I CORINTHIANS 10:12-13

Thanksgiving Reflections

Many times when we pray, we make requests of God. These are called prayers of petition. But another form of prayer, one that we sometimes overlook, is the prayer of thanksgiving. We should take time every day to thank God for the many blessings we receive. If you look, you will be able to find things in your life to thank God for, just as these Boys Town youth have.

Thank You, God, for the courage and ability to change myself. Thank You for the love and care that Boys Town has shown me and for all that I know and have learned. Thank You for helping me to be able to graduate and to learn right from wrong.

Thank You, too, for my two arms, two legs and healthy body. Thank You for helping me turn from a disastrous road to a road of success. Amen.

– MIKE

Thank You, God, for giving me the chance to be somebody. Even after I took advantage of it and screwed up, You gave me another chance. Thank You for being so understanding and forgiving.

– CARTER

Thank You, Lord, for changing my whole life. I am a better person now than when I was younger. Thank You for giving me such a beautiful place to live.

– JUSTIN

Thank You, God, for letting me participate in sports and be successful. Thank You for giving me good Family-Teachers who help me understand things and work with me. Thanks for giving me music to ease the pain I might be forced to face in life. But most of all, thank You for life.

– NIKIA

I am thankful, God, for sight, hearing, smelling, feeling, tasting and that I was lucky enough to have arms and legs. I thank God that I live in a free country.

– TOM

Thank You, God, for all the memories that I can look back on and learn from. Thank You for the people around me that help me and love me, that push me to do the best I can. Thank You for all the decisions You have let me make on my own. Thank You, God, for You.

– SHAWN

Thank You for all You have done for me. You brought light where there was none. You brought love where there was none. You gave me hope where it was needed. Thank You for giving me feelings to be able to love You and the people around me. Amen.

– TRISH

Thanks, Lord, for friends. Everyone needs friendship in life. Without friendship the world would be like hell. Some people think the earth is hell because they don't have love in their hearts and they don't have friends either. So, Lord, help those people to find love and friendship and make the world a better place to live in. Amen.

– JR

Dear Lord, I just want to take this time out to thank You for the game of basketball. I love the game so much that sometimes I'd rather just play basketball than do anything else. And I want to thank You for blessing me to be the best point-guard I can be. Another thing I really want to thank You for is girls, because without the girlfriend I have I don't know what I'd do, and thank You for making them so understanding. Amen.

— BRENT

My Lord,

I am thankful for the beautiful mountains You have created. There is nothing better than being able to go to the mountains and being free with the fresh air, and the many animals, trees and rocks. I thank You, Lord, for having such a place to go to be alone and free. Thank You for listening, Lord. Amen.

— HANNAH

If you have trouble putting your own thanks into words, read Psalm 100:

"Shout for joy to the Lord, all the earth. Serve the Lord with gladness; come before Him with joyful songs. Know that the Lord is God. It is He who made us, and we are His, we are His people, the sheep of His pasture.

"Enter His gates with thanksgiving and His courts with praise; give thanks to Him and praise His name. For the Lord is good and His love endures forever, His faithfulness continues through all generations."

Christmas Reflections

The following Christmas thoughts were written by our Boys Town youth:

Christmas means I have the chance to show my friends and family that no matter what is happening I can love them and give of myself to others in any way that can help. Christmas is also a time to thank God for His love and for food and clothes and a place to sleep.

— RYAN

It means sharing and caring, crying and laughing. There is a lot of that in our house, I was just blind to it. Now I will never take it for granted that I'm loved. I think God sent me here to open my eyes and see the light.

— PETER

Christmas means a time of giving and receiving. A time of joy and blessings. Most of all it is a time to worship our Lord.

— NICOLE

Christmas means to me love through all families, and sharing all you have, even if it's just a hug.

— PABLO

Christmas means two things to me – it is symbolic of a time for giving and a time for remembering. We are obligated to give during this Christmas season, not material objects but that which comes from the heart. We must give a part of ourselves to those we love and are close to us as well as those we do not know and are not as fortunate.

We must also remember to see past the glitter and lights which society has come to call "Christmas," and remember its true meaning. Christmas was set aside to commemorate the birth of Jesus Christ our Savior, who gave totally of Himself and asked nothing in return.

— DWAYNE

Christmas to me is a time of giving to one's own family and friends. A time to treat your fellow man with respect and kindness. A celebration of the birth of the Savior of the World.

— SHANTE

It means caring, caring for those in need.

It means sharing, sharing yourself to those who are lonely.

It means giving, giving your friendship to all people.

And joy, because Jesus Christ was born.

— ZACH

Before I came to Boys Town I never thought much about the "Christ" in Christmas. I knew that we celebrated Christ's birth on that day, but I never gave it any thought. I just thought about the presents and money that I would get from my family. I just thought about myself and what I was going to get. I wasn't thinking of what I could give.

Now that I am at Boys Town, I better understand the true meaning of Christmas. I still wonder and anticipate what I may be receiving under the tree on Christmas morning. But I also think about Christ now, and other people besides myself.

– JOHN

As for the meaning of Christmas for me, I'll speak to you from the heart. I come from a wonderful family, one that I've messed up. After driving my parents to do it, I was placed in several "out of home" placements. I have been away from my family a little over a year. This year I will go home the evening of my birthday and for three days at Christmas break. I am very happy and excited. I go about buying presents with renewed interest. I live at Boys Town now. I haven't been home for a while but eventually I will go home permanently. Till then, I have to make a happy life where I am. To me, Christmas is a time of family, love, peace and happiness.

– LEAH

Lenten Reflections

The following reflections on the characters of the passion of Jesus were written by Boys Town youth.

Jesus

Why do they not believe what I teach is real? This cross is heavy – my back is burning – my head is aching. The scorching sun is hot on my back! My task is almost completed and yet it's just beginning. My mother – I feel her sorrow in my heart. The pain she is feeling is strong. Peter is going to deny me. I love him so, but I forgive him for this is what it is all about. I give my life so you may have life.

– KATINA

Good Thief

I feel the good thief was a man who made mistakes like any other man. We too fall at times. I feel it's a good example that when we make mistakes like the thief, Jesus is willing to forgive those mistakes, as long as we're sorry.

– ELIJAH

Judas

Judas is like the everyday person. He didn't believe in Christ just as Peter didn't. Peter denied Jesus, but Judas betrayed Him. People today still deny Jesus and also do just as bad as Judas. Don't be a jerk like Judas.

– JESSICA

Jesus

Jesus is truly God's son. What he did for all of us was done out of pure love. I don't think I could have ever done what Jesus did. I do love Jesus. I have never seen him with these eyes but sometimes I feel Him in me. I might not follow Jesus the way He should be followed but I'm still trying. Maybe I'm still trying because of Jesus.

– TAYLOR

Mary

When people think of the passion of the Lord they usually think about the suffering that Jesus went through. They don't, however, think of how much Mary suffered. At least Jesus knew what was going to happen to Him and why.

But imagine a mother who sees her only son grow up to be scourged, mocked and crucified. She had to sit and watch her son die, with nothing she could do to help him and she barely understood why. But because she had faith in God she bore the suffering without complaint. She is a good example for us all – like a mother should be.

– SHAWNA

Pilate

Pilate was a very confused person. When Jesus was sentenced to death, Pilate sort of knew who Jesus was and wanted to set him free. The people wanted

Jesus to die and Pilate became confused and asked again who should be set free. Again the people said that the murderer should be set free.

Pilate didn't want to upset the people but he also didn't want Jesus to die. Pilate came to his decision that Jesus was to be crucified and he said that he would wash his hands of this sin. I think that Pilate was very confused and tried to make his decision too quickly. If he would have taken *time to think* about his decision, maybe Jesus wouldn't have been crucified. Even though Pilate washed his hands clean of his sin, I think he still felt very guilty about what he had done.

– BRETT

Peter

I know what you did was wrong and I also know you really didn't do it because you hated Jesus or anything like that. We are all humans, and we all can make mistakes from time to time. I know if you tell Jesus how sorry you are, he will surely forgive you. Remember to do the right thing whenever you can. And Jesus still loves you.

– BOOKER

Peter

I know that you must feel horrible right now, and I want you to know that I'm thinking of you now. It's not easy to stop feeling guilty. But your guilt won't change your actions. If you don't feel that you can live with your guilt, Peter, then please do something about it, so that you'll feel better. Try to act differently, don't deny what you really believe in. If you pray, then God will help you.

— AMBER

Graduation Reflections

The following reflections were written by Boys Town seniors at the time of their graduation.

When I first came here, I was really torn inside, and I did not care for anyone or anything. When I got settled into the home, my Family-Teachers helped me to believe in myself. For quite a while, I fought the system and was always trying to find the easy way out. After a while, with my friends, parents, and Family-Teachers' influence, I began to see a new light and path. One of the first and most important things I learned was how to rebuild relationships and keep them. This especially includes a relationship with God which helps me to start feeling complete with myself.

— ERIC

The most important thing I learned at Boys Town is to never give up. No matter how bad something may hurt or how hard the struggle, remember

Jesus' struggles were more. There is always some-one else in need who may be hurt. One way I will continue to live Father Flanagan's dream is to remember why he first started Boys Town; to pro-vide love, care and help to those in most need.

My prayer for those still attending Boys Town is that God will guide them and show them a real understanding and love for themselves, especially those who are hurt and those who hurt them. I pray they will be able to continue to keep going when things are at their worst. I pray they will believe that they are good people and a gift from God. I pray they will never give up and be able to teach and help others to believe and be happy.

— TINA

I am most thankful to Boys Town for giving me a second chance at getting my life together and help-ing me to work toward becoming the person I know I want to be. I am also thankful for everything I've learned and all the love I've shared over the years.

The most important thing I've learned while living here is that there are a lot of people who will help you, but nobody can help unless you want to help yourself. Everything you do or say, you're accountable for. Nobody can make you do anything. You have to want to do it. If you are to be successful and famous, you have to work for it. Nothing will ever be given to you free or easy.

– SHERRIE

The day I came to Boys Town, more than two years ago, I was mad at my family and glad to get out of my house. But as soon as I arrived here those feelings changed. I was homesick. I didn't want to be here. But someone told me to give this place a chance and I did.

The whole first year I was here I still wanted to just have fun. So I didn't learn much that year. Finally, something clicked inside me and told me that if I didn't succeed while I lived at Boys Town, then I had no future. I decided I should give "trying" a try.

Since that day I have succeeded in many different ways. I have grown close to God and to my family. I give Boys Town most of the credit for putting my life back into perspective, but I also give credit to my family who never gave up on me.

– SEAN

Boys Town means many things to me. Most of all it means opportunity. It gives you a chance to learn new ideas and to grow – both spiritually and physically. For anything to happen, you must want it. You may have trouble at first adjusting to Boys Town, but don't fight it. They can help you but you also have to help yourself. If you need help, ask. Everybody is more than willing to talk and help in any way they can.

– ROBERT

I am most thankful to Boys Town for giving me a place to live. I have been here for four years and am happy to have been a part of the girls program from the start. If it were not for Boys Town, I don't know where I would be living.

– MARY

I am very thankful to everyone here who picked me up when I was falling. I now have a future to look forward to and a good education. If it were not for Boys Town, I would have never finished school. But Boys Town made it happen for me.

– FARRELL

I arrived on a bright January day. When we drove through the main entrance, I told my cousin, "I'm going to be a new person with a new attitude on life when I leave from this entrance."

At that time I was placed in the home of two wonderful Family-Teachers. Through the months we became closer, just like a real family. We had many good times and a share of bad times. After we came back from vacation, one of the girls in our home had a bad attitude toward the rest of us. We sat in the living room talking to her about how we felt. Then after a while she came around. We've stuck together through the good times, but we got stronger through the bad times.

My prayer for those still attending is: let people help you. Don't be someone you're not, because everyone will pick up on it. I'm not going to tell you that you won't make mistakes, because you will. But it is what you learn from them that is the most important. I will never forget the people who have taken time to work with me and the other kids. Those people will always be in my heart.

— MARIA

Boys Town has changed my moral judgment. Before, I couldn't have cared about anyone but myself. If I couldn't get something out of people, I didn't want to associate with them. Today, I can see more in people than just what I can get from them. I can wait to judge people until I can see what their personalities portray, and not their appearance. For this I am thankful to Boys Town.

— JASON

I came on a Friday morning in October. I was really scared because it was going to be something new, and I really didn't want to go. But it was better than jail. I was really confused about life and I didn't have any respect or confidence in myself. I had a lot of questions about life. I did a lot of things because I thought that it was what I wanted or it was the answer to all my questions. Some of them were good things, but most of them got me in trouble. I was afraid to ask my parents or anyone else for help because I wanted to be independent and solve my problems by myself. Well, that didn't work. My first year was the hardest for me because I didn't want anyone to help me. I had gone this long doing things on my own and it was too hard to trust or ask for help from others.

Probably the two most important things I've learned while being here are that it is better to talk to someone about your problems or confusion than to keep it inside of you; and, if you don't believe in yourself, then how can anyone else believe in you. Over the years I have realized that these were the problems I had to work out. It took a while but with the help of my Family-Teachers, teachers and priests, I realize what I want out of life and who I am.

– JOSH

As I sit and reflect on my life here, I remember all of the opportunities that Boys Town has provided for me. The times when nothing was going right, when I thought that I would just give up, and then something that one of the kids or my Family-Teachers said would make all of the trouble worthwhile. The times when the people here would help when I was alone or afraid. And, most importantly, the chance Boys Town has given me to be someone.

I want to take this opportunity to thank each of you. Thank you for giving me a sense of being, a sense of responsibility, and most importantly, a future. I would like to leave the younger kids and next year's graduating class with one thought – you are the next generation. Work with Boys Town, as hard as it may be. Do your best, and never give up. Be proud of yourselves and the things that you do.

– KEVIN

When I first came, I was not happy to be here and I would play with the system hoping my stay here would be better. I realized that I wasn't working on my problems. I played a lot of games like always saying what my Family-Teachers wanted to hear.

When I started my senior year I was "happy." I would always say to myself, "This is my last year in high school" and then I got scared. I was happy and sad because this is my last year in high school. I was sad because I did not want to leave. I've learned a lot and I want to learn more. If I hadn't come I know I wouldn't be graduating this year. I wouldn't be accepted in a college. Boys Town has performed miracles with me.

– KATRINA

I can recall times when I was lonely and filled with despair. Having no one to turn to, I lost faith in myself. My understanding of life was distorted. Reaching out and finding only rejection brought forth a major downfall in my life. I doubted that there was a God. This same God that I doubted had taken the life of my lovely mother. As time progressed, I regressed. I watched myself deteriorate. The only thing that remained was the love that was once provided by my beloved mother. Knowing that she was still a part of my existence, I found the strength to reach out once more.

I extended my hand, hoping to find the same unconditional love like my mother had given me. I found that love and also a home here. Boys Town has not only given me love and understanding, it has given me faith, courage and the will to succeed. I encourage all of you to extend your hand and give Boys Town the opportunity to help you achieve your goals. Allow yourself to be open-minded and accept the benefits that Boys Town has to offer.

– EMMA

There must be someone up there who is looking over me and trying to do the best for me, because when I look back on all the years I have spent here, I see what I have accomplished. Father Flanagan said that there is no such thing as a bad boy. Well, I was a bad boy in a bad environment, getting a bad start on life. If you would have seen me then, you would have known what the Bible meant when it said man is born in sin and corruption. We all know that you can barely make it through this world without a college degree and if you don't have a high school one you surely can't. By dropping out in fifth grade, I surely didn't have a chance.

– JJ

The following introduction and poem were read by Lori, a student during our Eighth Grade Graduation ceremonies.

The poem I am about to read entitled, "Children Learn What They Live," has a very truthful message. I chose to read this poem because I feel it tells about the purpose of Boys Town. This poem particularly applies to the eighth grade class and our place of learning, Wegner School. The teachers and staff at Wegner have taught us many skills during our stay. Hopefully, through our high school years we will be able to stick together and help one another. As new students come, we can show them acceptance and friendship and help them succeed here.

I think we should especially thank our Family-Teachers. They have helped us as much as the teachers and staff have, and even more. They have helped me through many difficulties, have stuck with me through good and bad, and have always been there for me. For this I love them very much.

Please pay close attention to this poem. It has a very special meaning to me and I hope that it will mean something to you, too.

Children Learn What They Live

When children live with hostility,
   they learn to fight.
When children live with ridicule,
   they learn to be shy.
When children live with shame,
   they learn to feel guilty.
When children live with tolerance,
   they learn to be patient.
When children live with encouragement,
   they learn to be confident.
When children live with security,
   they learn to have faith.
When children live with fairness,
   they learn justice.
When children live with praise,
   they learn to appreciate.
When children live with approval,
   they learn to like themselves.
When children live with acceptance
   and friendship,
      they learn to find love in the world.

Father Flanagan
Speaks
to Youth

Father Edward J. Flanagan
Founder of Boys Town

On Homesickness

Father Flanagan said:

"We all suffer from homesickness, even when we get old and have been away from home many, many years. I too get homesick from time to time. You will always have good memories of your homes, along with the bad ones. Don't forget these memories, but rather hold onto them and cherish them. Use the good memories as a base for what you want in the future, the bad memories for what you don't want. Don't let these good memories be a reason to make you feel down. They should make you feel good.

"Leabeg House, ancestral home of the Flanagans in Ireland was not unlike other rural homes of the day in Southern County Roscommon. Its walls were of white limestone, with a rough exterior and thatched roof.

"There were eleven of us children, four boys and seven girls. Alexander Graham Bell's telephone was still a curiosity. The automobile was unknown, as was the airplane, the radio, the "talkies." Nevertheless, evenings were neither long nor dull. We had a fine melodeon, a piano, a violin, a flute and a concertina. Each of us was encouraged to play at least one instrument and there was scarcely an Irish folk song we didn't know.

"Family life today is threatened by the tempo of pleasure-mad living. People are so busy making a living or seeking social preference that they have no time for their children. We need to realize that the greatest advantage any boy or girl can have is the advantage of a good, religious home.

"The home should be a sanctuary of love and religious idealism. It should be a place where people live, where the cares and worries of the office are forgotten, where the laughter of children is heard, where one can find time for companionship and meditation. This is what home means to me. It is our refuge from the frustrations of the world outside, the child's haven of happiness and dreams."

– "THE PERFECT HOME, WHAT HOME MEANS TO ME,"
MAY 14, 1947

Prayer When Feeling Homesick

Father in Heaven, I don't know anyone here. You're the only one I can talk to that doesn't ask a lot of questions, like; "Who are you?" 'Where are you from?" or 'What's your name?" I am not sure why I am here or why I can't be somewhere else. Help me to understand some of the reasons. Help me to learn not to let it bother me so much. Give me some peace of mind so I can hear your words clearly.

Father, there have been some "bad times" in my life. I've been hurt. I won't treat anyone else that way. In fact, I know You want me to help You change this world for the better. Maybe there will be other tough people and places in the future. But I know that they will not keep me from Your love for me. For that I thank you most of all. I wait in hope for tomorrow. Amen.

On Sickness

Father Flanagan said:

"When we're not feeling well, perhaps so sick we have to go to the hospital, fear is perhaps the strongest opponent we must deal with. Fear of things that endanger existence (life) or well-being are important for our survival and personal development. Just as fear of poverty is an incentive for thrift, or fear of failure spurs us to work hard, fear of disease should primarily only inspire get-well measures.

"A wholesome kind of fear is an aid against many human weaknesses which plague the individual and stand in the way of his progress toward his fullest possible self-realization. The person who lacks this kind of fear invites disaster.

"But not all fear is wholesome. On the contrary, most of our fears are not only needless but also harmful, and are a source of grievous mental ills. Fear that serves no useful purpose, which interferes with essential habits and does not stimulate to action or belief, destroys rather than promotes mental health. It disrupts the way we think and burns up nervous energy necessary for getting better.

"The unfamiliarity of the child, due to his lack of experience, and his active imagination also makes one an easy victim of fears. Not only does the child believe it when parents say that if you do not go to sleep the bogeyman will get you, but also, childish imagination calls up all sorts of anxieties and dreads. By stressing the positive it is possible to avoid these suggestions of fear.

"The fears of the little child seem trivial to the adult. This is because the adult understands what the child does not. Never should fathers and mothers laugh at the child when he or she is afraid even when they know the fears are harmless. To do so is to add to confusion. The way to overcome fear is to be familiar with the object of fear (illness, hospital, etc.). This has to be done gradually, not all at one time, and not by force. Once understood, the basis of fear vanishes, the child is no longer afraid."

– "Boys Town Times," February 27, 1948

Prayer When Sickness Overcomes Us

I came into this world with nothing, Lord. Everything I have is Yours. I am only a pilgrim on the road to my true home in heaven. If I "take" happiness from Your hand freely as Your gift, must I not also be willing to "take" the sadness or sorrow that comes along? I will always love You, give You praise and thank You all of my life, dear Lord. I know there is one thing which can never be taken from me, and this is Your love. And there is one thing I would never let anyone take from me, my love for You.

When things go wrong, like they are now, all I have to think about is the future. I will be with You one day, sooner or later, forever. The one prayer I have is to live in Your house, both here on earth and afterwards in heaven. Anyone who would want to take this dream from me is not my friend or Yours, but a friend of the "evil one." Let me keep myself far away from that one.

The Lord gives, and the Lord takes away. Holy is His name. Amen.

On Discrimination

Father Flanagan said:

"Today, more perhaps, than ever before, we must bend our energies to the salvation of our youth. The country is alive with 'isms' and each one is making a strong bid for the support of our citizens of tomorrow. The appeal they make must be offset by an appeal of our own. Youth needs to be trained in citizenship – it needs to be taught what citizenship means.

"There is room for but one 'ism' in this country, and that one is Americanism. We want neither a black-shirt, or red flag, nor a brownshirt in this country. What we want, and what we must preserve, is democracy. I see no danger in our own system, dedicated to individualistic happy lives, and free from regimentation and repression. I see neither weakness nor folly in a system which vests the right of government where it belongs, in the people. I see no disaster threatening us because of any particular race, creed or color.

"But I do see danger for all in an ideology which discriminates against anyone politically or economically because he was born into the wrong race, has skin of the wrong color, or worships at the wrong altar. I am happy and the whole world should be profoundly grateful that American boys are armed with baseball bats and not rifles, that they are taught to throw baseballs and not grenades.

"American youth has much for which to be grateful. Only cast your eyes abroad and you will see it – youngsters being trained and regimented with but a single, horrible destiny. Death on the battlefield – for the glory and aggrandizement of selfish, senseless state."

– Address delivered in Cleveland, Ohio, on July 30, 1939
for National Amateur Baseball Day

Prayer When Feeling Attacked by Others

God, I feel like some people are against me. I see that we are all alike. You made us all Your children. But others look for differences. I feel sorry for them and pray for them. But no one could ever make me believe You do not love us all the same. I wish there were not evil in the world, but it will never defeat You, and I don't want it to make me sad.

I have been hurt by what others have said or thought. I am trying to get along but I am sometimes afraid. It's often hard for me to go out and I want so much to be a part of this world You have created.

I need Your help. Please strengthen and bring out even more of Your goodness within me. Let those who are doing bad things to me and others see the glory and power of Your ways. If they can not change, help those who work for Your justice move quickly against them. Most of all, be with me at those times most difficult, because I know if You are there, I will be okay. With You by my side, how can I be afraid. Amen.

On Misuse of Sex

Father Flanagan said:

"The way modern novelists and script writers toss the thing around, one would think that there was little more to life than sex, and that sex is all of love. That is far from the case. Love means sacrifice and mutual devotion. It means a sharing of experiences, both joys and sorrows, and it means constructing a satisfying life out of all that comes the mutual way of the lovers.

"Isn't sacrifice the real measure of love? It's not what you do for yourself that proves your love for another! The sexual impulse in a boy or girl gives rise to genuine love, and genuine love finds completion in the sexual act. But! You should never confuse the two.

"Marriages go on the rocks because people don't realize the nature, and the demands, and the responsibilities of genuine love, and they mistake the sexual variety for the real thing. Genuine love in married life comes only to two people who are mutually and supremely unselfish.

"Where should the sexual impulse be fitted into your own life? Accept it now, as a gift from the Creator to you. Realize that He put it there for a purpose, and that the purpose is not your selfish gratification. I cannot ask you to forget it! I admit that this would be impossible. I know that you can keep it within proper bounds, and I can promise you that if you do, you will have prepared the finest base upon which to rest a marriage, when you are trained and educated and able, in every respect, to contract one.

"You have to lose your self and your selfish interests to make a success of married life. If you learn to lose that selfishness as you grow up, will you not be better prepared to make the sacrifices marriage demands? I know that you will."

– "FATHER FLANAGAN'S ESSAYS ON BOYS"
(UNPUBLISHED), "A TALK TO A BOY"

Prayer on Proper Use of Sex

Dear Jesus, You were born into this world surrounded by love. So many loved You. Angels, Shepherds and Kings were near You. Your mother, Mary, loved everyone about her, and she especially loved You, in such a faithful way. An evil king, Herod, wanted to kill You, and lots of people did not care a bit about You.

I used to think that no one really loved me, and I used my body (and other peoples' bodies) to try to pretend I could love. But You told me that wasn't the right way. I don't have to let people touch me in bad ways to hear the words "I love you."

Jesus, it's hard to break old habits sometimes. And sometimes I just get confused. Other people try to confuse me. And what's worse, I can lie to myself about what's right and wrong. I try to confuse myself.

I pray that You send me people to love and that I can love others, as You want me. I know You will, because no one cares for me like You do. Right now I want to also pray that You make me smart. Send me enough grace to know when someone tries to confuse me, and please let me be at least smart enough to not confuse and hurt myself. I'm happy though, deep down, because You love me. I love You, Jesus. Amen.

On Violence

Father Flanagan said:

"Long before psychologists told us the way to cure a bad habit is to replace it with a good habit, Christ taught that we should overcome evil by doing good.

"If we want peace and the blessings of peace for ourselves and our neighbors, then we must look to the Prince of Peace. If we want to live in a good world then we must help make it that kind of a world by our acts and prayers. If we want good will to reign, then we must see first that we are people of good will.

"How the heart starves for the happiness that comes with sacrifice for others through love of God! And what a feast it enjoys at Christmas time when the cares and worries over the material things of life are lost in the wholehearted exuberance which marks the Christmas spirit of charity and love for all!

"But what benefit will our scientific learning bring us, if, because God has been left out, we end up with an atomic bomb and our Christian civilization a shambles?"

– "FATHER FLANAGAN'S BOYS' HOME JOURNAL,"
DECEMBER, 1946

Prayer When Feeling Abused

Lord Jesus, I owe You so much and You give me everything. I need to now repay Your mercy. How could I be so stupid – only You can decide what's best for us all. I thought I was hurt and I just wanted to hurt others. No one has the right to hurt anyone, yet I did.

You are a God who could destroy anyone and everyone if You wanted to. But You choose only to love us. I guess that's what true strength is all about. Nothing can defeat the power of Your love. You are "all goodness." Nothing can defeat Your love within me.

But You know everything so You know I too am really good. I want to be a good person. I'll always need Your help – so now I ask for it. Let me see and hear those things I need to see and hear to do only good. Let me use the strength You've given me to be of help to You, Lord Jesus. I want to serve You. Thank You for helping me.

On Stealing

Father Flanagan said:

"Theft has at all times been looked upon as a crime and thieves are always branded with public contempt and punished severely when found guilty. The thief does not even think well of himself since he always seeks out the darkness of the night to execute his projects and will not suffer anyone to call him a thief.

"Ill-gotten goods do not generally make a person rich. 'My curse shall come to the house of the thief, and it shall be consumed,' says Holy Writ. And even if a person were to prosper, what would it avail you if you should lose your immortal soul. One single reverse of fortune may rob you of all your possessions, and you must leave them sooner or later. What counts above all other things are the riches of Heaven which are eternal.

"My dear children, be very mindful then of this Commandment of God. Respect the property of others. It belongs to them. Do not injure that property in any way. "Should you ever be so unfortunate as to be guilty of this sin of stealing, then strive to make restitution to the best of your ability, and ask God for forgiveness.

"Beware of falling into the habit of taking little things which do not belong to you. This may become a very serious defect in your character. For you know by repeated acts you may some day begin taking big things, and earn for yourself a very bad name, be a disgrace to yourself and to your family, and may even thereby lose your immortal soul."

– "FATHER FLANAGAN'S BOYS' HOME JOURNAL,"
JULY, 1930

Prayer When
I'm Sorry I've Stolen

Jesus, I feel like I've been tried and accused of being bad. People might even think that I am bad. Maybe the things I did were bad, but I am not. It's too late to change the past. But I want You to know I do feel sorry for anything I ever stole – money, material goods, things from stores and, even worse, when I stole someone else's dream of what their life should be like.

Right now I want You to know I want to be good – from this day on. I know I can best do this by taking You as my Savior. Not by wearing a sign or badge of any kind, but by living the way You want me to live.

The Good Thief learned this while dying. Please let me learn it while living for You. You've never stopped being my best friend. From now on, I want to be Your best friend. From this day on, I want to feel that You are with me always. Amen.

On Drinking

Father Flanagan said:

"Do you want to control alcoholism in your life? One important way is to gain emotional stability. Another is to discover purpose and direction in your life. By contrast, when the emotions are unbridled or we lose purpose in our life, alcoholism might be grasped at as the remedy (wrongly).

"Control of the emotions does not mean that they should be throttled. It means that they should be directed and modified in keeping with the needs to be met. One who is a slave of his emotions lives in a wretched existence. But one who makes the emotions his servant finds them an invaluable possession.

"A characteristic of emotional instability is the tendency to run away from reality instead of facing it honestly and courageously. The unhappy person is continually seeking an escape. One of the first things the youth should learn, therefore, is that it does not pay to run away from problems. This can be accomplished by encouraging willingness to face facts and by helping the youth to solve the problem.

"Finding a definite purpose in your life aids any person because it provides a plan of action which enables you to avoid the main distractions of life. It makes possible a focal point for your attention. When your attention is centered upon one aim or goal to the exclusion of all other goals, the effectiveness of your will is increased.

"Having a definite purpose or aim makes it possible for us to live more fully in the present. It gives significance to the job at hand. Only by doing the task immediately before us are we able to reach our objective. The person who dwells in the past, like the person who lives too much in the future, gets little done. He misses the significance of the present."

– "Boys Town Times,"
January 23 and April 9, 1948

Prayer When I Want
to Stay Sober

Creator of all things, God of heaven and earth, God of sun and moon, light and day, and all the creatures who live...God of me. You are so great and strong and I am so weak. Sometimes I feel that I am some-one else, or that something else has control of me. Once, I just could not stand it any longer and I only wanted to drink, to drug myself and to forget.

That's because we are all so weak. But You, God, are the strong one, I know that with Your help I can be anything I want to be. I too can be strong. Strong enough to say no to what is ugly.

How can drinking and drugs be considered beautiful, when people do ugly things when they drink or "do" drugs. You love me, God, and I know You didn't make me to act like that. The world doesn't need any more alcoholics or addicts. What the world does need are more friends of Christ, people to help Him rebuild this world. Right now I want to be holy, like You, Jesus, and to be with You. Help me. Amen.

On Lying

Father Flanagan said:

"A habit, my dear children, is nothing else than the result of repeated acts, whether they be good or bad. After doing a certain thing time and time again, our will becomes subject to that action, and we get so that eventually we do it whether we wish to or not.

"For instance, a child who has trained himself to always tell the truth, regardless of the circumstances or results, will eventually acquire the habit of truthfulness, and the virtue will become so firmly a part of him that no temptation of loss or gain could compel him ever to swerve from the truth. On the other hand, a child who tells lies frequently, acquires that habit and becomes a slave to it, and later in life will become just a common liar."

– "Father Flanagan's Boys' Home Journal,"
May, 1930

Prayer When I've Lied

Jesus, I sometimes do not tell the truth about some things. When I do this, I know it hurts people. It is hardest on me because it keeps me away from You. It makes You sad too. I am most sorry for that. You have given me everything and look how I behave.

I need some help with this. I need to be smarter, if other people are trying to talk me into lying. I need to learn that after all You mean more to me than anyone or anything. I also need to have courage, if it seems telling the truth goes against what others say.

I need to be strong with this weakness in myself. I know that in weakness, there is strength when we know it and let You heal it. I turn this over to You. I promise to try to love You more. Make me a closer brother/sister to You. This is what I really want, and You know if I'm telling the truth – when no one else might be sure. Amen.

On Bad Language and Bad Manners

Father Flanagan said:

"The knack of getting along with others is an invaluable asset. Speaking well and avoiding vulgar words must be a part of these skills. Some people do this well, they are good 'mixers.' They make friends easily; they gain recognition and advancement more readily. And what they can do, others also can do, if they try.

"However, the habit of good language goes deeper than surface appearances. It is rooted in consideration for the other person. Every act of courtesy is a recognition of the rights of the person to whom courtesy is shown. Rudeness of manners or language suggests lack of social awareness. It means the individual is self-centered and not thoughtful of others. Although no offense may be intended, the lack of consideration creates prejudice against him or her.

"Bad language as a result of losing only makes everyone stay apart. A good sport shakes hands whether he or she wins or loses. What kind of world would we have if men and women ignored rules of social custom? People would be getting in each other's way constantly, stepping on each other's toes, and generally making life miserable for themselves and those around them.

"The need for more emphasis upon good language in preparing the boy for life has been increased by the demands of our more complex society. Never has the youth had greater opportunities than today, but never have the requirements for success been more difficult. And among these requirements is consideration for the other person expressed in the way we speak to that person."

– "BOYS TOWN TIMES,"
OCTOBER 24, 1947 AND APRIL 23, 1948

Prayer for Help with Bad Language

Lord, please help me get rid of this bad habit – my foul language. When I was little I heard people talk like this and I thought it would make me seem grown-up, or maybe I just wanted to be like those people. But it's time for a change. I look around and I see how language like this is terrible. When people lose their tempers, get mad or are unhappy, it gets worse. People who are truly happy with themselves, are at peace, and don't talk like this.

If I get angry, talking like this doesn't help at all. When I talk like this and am around others who do, we just all bring each other down. In the end I go away feeling cheap. Who would really want to get close to me the way I talk? Not the kind of people I want around me always.

I want You to make Your home with me, God. You will only live in a clean home – so that's how I want to make myself. It isn't as hard as it looks, I know. I also know I can really be a friend to those around me by trying to help them talk correctly, too. Lord, You give me all good things. You wouldn't make anything bad. Help me to make myself good again, the way I should be. Let me pray to You always, with a clean mouth. Amen.

Traditional Catholic Prayers

Dowd Memorial Chapel,
Boys Town Campus

The Sign of the Cross

We make the Sign of the Cross by touching with the right hand:

The forehead, saying, "In the Name of the Father,"

Then the chest, adding, "and of the Son,"

And then from the left shoulder to the right, while saying, "and of the Holy Spirit. Amen."

The Sign of the Cross shows that we are Christians because it expresses our belief in the chief mysteries of our Catholic faith: the mystery of the Blessed Trinity, the mystery of the Incarnation, and the mystery of the Redemption. The words we say show that God is One in Three Divine Persons. The cross we make reminds us that Jesus Christ, the Son of God, died for us on the Cross.

The Lord's Prayer

Our Father, who art in heaven,

hallowed be thy name;

Thy kingdom come;

Thy will be done on earth as it is in heaven.

Give us this day our daily bread;

and forgive us our trespasses

as we forgive those who trespass against us;
and lead us not into temptation,
but deliver us from evil. Amen.

The Hail Mary

Hail Mary, full of grace,
The Lord is with thee;
blessed are thou among women;
and blessed is the fruit of thy womb, Jesus.
Holy Mary, Mother of God,
pray for us sinners,
now and at the hour of our death. Amen.

Glory to the Father

Glory be to the Father,
and to the Son, and to the Holy Spirit.
As it was in the beginning,
is now, and ever shall be,
world without end. Amen.

The Apostles' Creed

I believe in God, the Father Almighty, Creator of heaven and earth; and in Jesus Christ, His only son, Our Lord, who was conceived by the Holy Spirit, born of the Virgin Mary, suffered under Pontius Pilate; was crucified, died, and was buried. He descended into hell; the third day He rose again from the dead. He ascended into heaven, sits at the right hand of God, the Father Almighty; from thence He shall come to judge the living and the dead. I believe in the Holy Spirit, the Holy Catholic Church, the communion of saints, the forgiveness of sins, the resurrection of the body, and life everlasting. Amen.

The Beatitudes

When He saw the crowds, He went up on the mountainside. After He had sat down, His disciples gathered around Him, and He began to teach them:

How blest are the poor in spirit: the reign of
   God is theirs.

Blest are the lowly; they shall inherit the land.

Blest are they who hunger and thirst for
   holiness; they shall have their fill.

Blest are they who show mercy; mercy shall be
theirs.

Blest are the single-hearted for they shall see God.

Blest too the peacemakers; they shall be called
sons of God.

Blest are those persecuted for holiness' sake; the
reign of God is theirs.

Blest are you when they insult you and persecute
you and utter every kind of slander against you
because of me. Be glad and rejoice, for your
reward is great in heaven; they persecuted the
prophets before you in the very same way.

– MATTHEW 5:1-12

Anima Christi

Soul of Christ sanctify me;
Body of Christ save me;
Blood of Christ inebriate me;
Water from the side of Christ wash me;
Passion of Christ strengthen me;
O good Jesus hear me;
Within Your wounds hide me;
Never permit me to be separated from You;
From the evil one protect me,

At the hour of my death call me,
And bid me come to You
That with Your saints
I may praise You forever. Amen

– St. Ignatius

The Confiteor

I confess to Almighty God, to blessed Mary ever Virgin, to blessed Michael the Archangel, to blessed John the Baptist, to the holy Apostles Peter and Paul, and to all the saints, that I have sinned exceedingly in thought, word and deed, through my fault, through my fault, through my most grievous fault. Therefore, I beseech blessed Mary ever Virgin, blessed Michael the Archangel, blessed John the Baptist, the holy Apostles Peter and Paul, and all the saints, to pray to the Lord our God for me.

May Almighty God have mercy on me, and forgive me my sins, and bring me to everlasting life. Amen. May the Almighty and Merciful Lord grant me pardon, absolution, and remission of all my sins. Amen.

Act of Contrition

O my God, I am heartily sorry for having offended You, and I detest all my sins, because I dread the loss of heaven and the pains of hell, but most of all because they offend You, my God, who are all-good and deserving of all my love. I firmly resolve, with the help of Your grace, to confess my sins, to do penance, and to amend my life. Amen.

The Ten Commandments of God

1. I, the Lord, am your God.
   You shall not have other gods besides me.

2. You shall not take the name of the Lord,
   your God, in vain.

3. Remember to keep holy the Lord's day.

4. Honor your father and your mother.

5. You shall not kill.

6. You shall not commit adultery.

7. You shall not steal.

8. You shall not bear false witness
   against your neighbor.

9. You shall not covet your neighbor's wife.

10. You shall not covet anything that
    belongs to your neighbor.

The Works of Mercy

Spiritual Works of Mercy

1. To admonish the sinner
2. To instruct the ignorant
3. To counsel the doubtful
4. To comfort the sorrowful
5. To bear wrongs patiently
6. To forgive all injuries
7. To pray for the living and the dead

Corporal Works of Mercy

1. To feed the hungry
2. To give drink to the thirsty
3. To clothe the naked
4. To visit the imprisoned
5. To shelter the homeless
6. To visit the sick
7. To bury the dead

Act of Faith

O my God, I firmly believe that You are one God in three Divine Persons, the Father, the Son, and the Holy Spirit. I believe that your Divine Son became man and died for our sins, and who will come to judge the living and the dead. I believe these and all the truths which the Holy Catholic Church teaches, because You have revealed them, who can neither deceive nor be deceived. Amen.

Act of Hope

O my God, relying on Your infinite goodness and promises, I hope to obtain pardon of my sins, the help of Your grace, and life everlasting, through the merits of Jesus Christ, my Lord and Redeemer. Amen.

Act of Love

O my God, I love You above all things, with my whole heart and soul, because You are all good and worthy of my love. I love my neighbor as myself for love of You. I forgive all who have injured me, and I ask pardon of all whom I have injured. Amen.

Morning Offering

O Jesus, through the immaculate heart of Mary, I offer You my prayers, works, joys and sufferings of this day, for all the intentions of Your Sacred Heart, in union with the holy sacrifice of the Mass throughout the world, in reparation for my sins, for the intentions of all our associates, and in particular for the intention recommended this month by the Holy Father.

The Magnificat

My soul magnifies the Lord, and my spirit
   rejoices in God my Savior;

Because He has regarded the lowliness of
   His handmaid;

for, behold, henceforth all generations shall
   call me blessed;

Because He who is mighty has done great things
   for me, and holy is His name;

And His mercy is from generation to generation
   on those who fear Him.

He has shown with His arm, He has scattered
   the proud in the conceit of their heart.

He has put down the mighty from their thrones,
   and has exalted the lowly.

He has filled the hungry with good things, and the
   rich He has sent away empty.

He has given help to Israel, His servant, mindful
of His mercy –

Even as He spoke to our fathers – to Abraham and
to His posterity forever.

The Memorare

Remember, O most gracious Virgin Mary, that
never was it known that anyone who fled to your
protection, implored your help or sought your
intercession, was left unaided.

Inspired by this confidence, I fly to you, O Virgin of
Virgins, my mother. To you I come; before you I
stand, sinful and sorrowful.

O Mother of the Word Incarnate, despise not my
petitions, but in your mercy, hear and answer me.
Amen.

– St. Bernard

The Angel of the Lord
(Angelus)

During the year (outside of Paschal Season)

The Angel of the Lord declared unto Mary,
And she conceived of the Holy Spirit. Hail Mary.
Behold the handmaid of the Lord.
Be it done unto me according to Your Word.
  Hail Mary.

And the Word was made flesh.
And dwelt among us. Hail Mary.
Pray for us, O holy Mother of God,
That we may be made worthy of the
promises of Christ.

Let us pray. Pour forth, we beg You, O Lord, Your grace into our hearts: that we, to whom the Incarnation of Christ Your Son was made known by the message of an Angel, may by His Passion and Cross be brought to the glory of His Resurrection. Through the same Christ our Lord. Amen.

During Paschal Season

Queen of Heaven, rejoice, alleluia:
For He whom you merited to bear, alleluia,
Has risen, as He said, alleluia.
Pray for us to God, alleluia.
Rejoice and be glad, O Virgin Mary, alleluia.
Because the Lord is truly risen, alleluia.

Let us pray. O God, who by the Resurrection of Your Son, our Lord Jesus Christ, granted joy to the whole world: grant, we beg You, that through the intercession of the Virgin Mary, His Mother, we may lay hold of the joys of eternal life. Through the same Christ our Lord. Amen.

— ROMAN BREVIARY

Prayer to Our Lady
in the Sorrows of Life

Hail, holy Queen, Mother of mercy, Hail, our life, our sweetness and our hope! To you do we cry, poor banished children of Eve! To you do we send up our sighs, mourning and weeping in this vale of tears. Turn then, most gracious advocate, Your eyes of mercy toward us; And, after this our exile, show us the blessed fruit of your womb, Jesus. O clement, O loving, O sweet Virgin Mary! Pray for us, O holy Mother of God, that we may be made worthy of the promises of Christ.

Grace Before Meals

Bless us, O Lord, and these Thy gifts, which we are about to receive from Thy bounty, through Christ, our Lord. Amen.

Grace After Meals

We give Thee thanks, Almighty God, for all Thy gifts and benefits who live and reign forever. And may the souls of the faithful departed through the mercy of God rest in peace. Amen.

Prayer of St. Francis

Lord, Make me an instrument of Thy peace.
Where there is hatred, Let me show love;
Where there is injury, pardon;
Where there is doubt, faith;
Where there is despair, hope;
Where there is darkness, light;
Where there is sadness, joy.

O Divine Master, Grant that I may seek
Not so much to be consoled, as to console;
To be understood, as to understand;
To be loved, as to love;
For it is in giving that we receive;
It is in pardoning that we are pardoned;
It is in dying that we are born to eternal life.
Amen.

A Universal Prayer

(Attributed to Pope Clement Xl)

This prayer is given in the back of the Sacramentary. It is an excellent summary of developmental needs and potentials seen in the light of the Gospel.

Lord, I believe in You: increase my faith.
I trust in You: strengthen my trust.
I love You: let me love You more and more.
I am sorry for my sins: deepen my sorrow.

I worship You as my first beginning,
I long for You as my last end,
I praise You as my constant helper,
and call on You as my loving protector.

Guide me by Your wisdom,
correct me with Your justice,
comfort me with Your mercy,
protect me with Your power.

I offer You, Lord, my thoughts: to be fixed
    on You;
my words: to have You for their theme;
my actions: to reflect my love for You;
my sufferings: to be endured for Your
    greater glory.

I want to do what You ask of me:
in the way You ask,
for as long as You ask,
because You ask it.

Lord, enlighten my understanding,
strengthen my will,
purify my heart,
and make me holy.

Help me to repent of my past sins
and to resist temptation in the future.
Help me to rise above my human weaknesses
and to grow stronger as a Christian.

Let me love You, my Lord and my God,
and see myself as I really am:
a pilgrim in this world,
a Christian called to respect and love
all whose lives I touch,
those in authority over me,
of those under my authority,
my friends and my enemies.

Help me to conquer anger with gentleness,
greed by generosity,
apathy by fervor.
Help me to forget myself
and reach out toward others.

Make me prudent in planning,
courageous in taking risks.
Make me patient in suffering,
unassuming in prosperity.

Keep me, Lord, attentive at prayer,
temperate in food and drink,
diligent in my work,
firm in my good intentions.

Let my conscience be clear,
my conduct without fault,
my speech blameless,
my life well ordered.

How to Make a Confession

Step 1: **Preparation for Confession:** Through prayer and reflection, make a good examination of your conscience.
Then say silently your act of contrition. Wait quietly for your turn.

Step 2: **Greeting:** Enter the confessional and make the Sign of the Cross. Tell the priest when you last went to confession.

Step 3: **Confession of Sins:** Here you humbly tell your sins to the Lord and His servant, the priest.

Step 4: **Penance:** The priest will then give you a penance to be said after you leave the confessional.

Step 5: **Expression of Sorrow:** You now make a good act of contrition.

Step 6: **Absolution:** God now gives you forgiveness of your sins through the words said by the priest: "I absolve you from your sins in the name of the Father and the Son and the Holy Spirit."

Step 7: **Proclamation of Praise of God:**
"The Lord has freed you from your sins. Go in peace." (Said by the priest.)
"Thanks, Father." (Said by you.)

Remember: Every confession is unique. This is just a sample of how to go to confession. If at any time during your confession you need help, the priest is always more than willing to help you.

Examination of Conscience

1. Have I failed to pray as I should?
   Have I given up on God at times?

2. Have I cussed and sworn and taken the good Lord's name in vain?

3. Have I missed Mass on Sundays or holy days?

4. Have I failed to honor my mother and father?
   Have I allowed myself to feel guilty when in fact I was abused physically or sexually?

5. Have I tried to hurt myself or others?

6. Have I used fights and threats to get my way?

7. Have I done harm to myself by using alcohol or drugs? Have I encouraged others to do so?

8. Have I neglected to give my body the proper care and food it needs to be healthy? Have I tried to hurt myself or others?

9. Have I failed to use my brain to the best of my ability?

10. Have I failed to play, laugh, and enjoy life?

11. Have I failed to look for the good things that happen each day (someone's smile, a good grade, a sunny day) and be thankful for it?

12. Have I done sexual things I should not have done?

13. Have I stolen from others? Have I returned the things I have stolen?

14. Have I cheated on tests or homework?

15. Have I lied to avoid the consequences of things I have done? Do I blame other students or adults when I'm in trouble instead of taking responsibility for my actions or reactions?

16. Have I lied?

17. Am I harming others by spreading gossip?

18. Am I harming anyone by excluding them from my circle of friends? Am I harming myself by only associating with a small group of friends?

19. Am I harming myself by not listening to other ideas of positive ways of acting? Am I stubborn?

20. Am I harming myself by not strengthening my relationship with God through prayer and participation in the Sacraments? Have I taken time to pray and develop a closer relationship with God?

21. Have I used other people? Have I pretended to be friends with others so I can share in their popularity?

22. Have I wanted someone's friendship so badly that I have not been brave enough to say that his or her actions or ideas are wrong or harmful?

23. Have I been selfish?

24. Have I been too hard on myself? Have I failed to forgive myself?

25. Do I have a hard time saying I'm sorry?

26. Do I let the Lord love me?

The Mysteries of the Rosary

The Joyful Mysteries

The Annunciation
The Visitation
The Nativity
The Presentation
The Finding in the Temple

The Sorrowful Mysteries

The Agony in the Garden
The Scourging at the Pillar
The Crowning with Thorns
The Carrying of the Cross
The Crucifixion

The Glorious Mysteries

The Resurrection
The Ascension
The Descent of the Holy Spirit
The Assumption of Mary into Heaven
The Coronation of Mary as Queen of Heaven

How to Say the Rosary

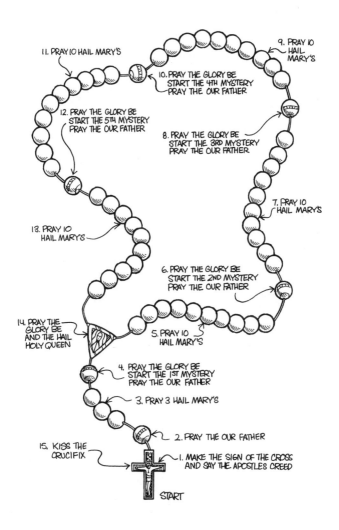

11. PRAY 10 HAIL MARY'S

9. PRAY 10 HAIL MARY'S

10. PRAY THE GLORY BE START THE 4TH MYSTERY PRAY THE OUR FATHER

12. PRAY THE GLORY BE START THE 5TH MYSTERY PRAY THE OUR FATHER

8. PRAY THE GLORY BE START THE 3RD MYSTERY PRAY THE OUR FATHER

7. PRAY 10 HAIL MARY'S

13. PRAY 10 HAIL MARY'S

6. PRAY THE GLORY BE START THE 2ND MYSTERY PRAY THE OUR FATHER

14. PRAY THE GLORY BE AND THE HAIL HOLY QUEEN

5. PRAY 10 HAIL MARY'S

4. PRAY THE GLORY BE START THE 1ST MYSTERY PRAY THE OUR FATHER

3. PRAY 3 HAIL MARY'S

2. PRAY THE OUR FATHER

15. KISS THE CRUCIFIX

1. MAKE THE SIGN OF THE CROSS AND SAY THE APOSTLES CREED

START

Traditional
Protestant
Prayers

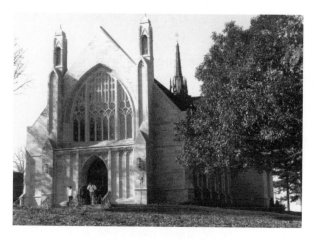

Chambers Protestant Chapel,
Boys Town Campus

Morning Prayer

I thank Thee, my heavenly Father, through Jesus Christ, Thy dear Son, that Thou has kept me this night from all harm and danger; and I pray Thee that Thou wouldst keep me this day also from sin and every evil, that all my doings and life may please Thee. For into Thy hands I commend myself, my body and soul, and all things. Let Thy holy angel be with me, that the wicked Foe may have no power over me. Amen.

– MARTIN LUTHER'S "SMALL CATECHISM"

Evening Prayer

I thank Thee, my heavenly Father, through Jesus Christ, Thy dear Son, that Thou hast graciously kept me this day; and I pray Thee that Thou wouldst forgive me all my sins where I have done wrong, and graciously keep me this night. For into Thy hands I commend myself, my body and soul, and all things. Let Thy holy angel be with me, that the wicked Foe may have no power over me. Amen.

– MARTIN LUTHER'S "SMALL CATECHISM"

Prayer Before Meals

Come, Lord Jesus, be our Guest, and let these gifts to us be blest. Amen.

The eyes of all wait upon You, O Lord, and You give them their meal in due season; You open Your hand and satisfy the desire of all living things. Amen.

Prayer After Meals

Oh give thanks unto the Lord for He is good, and His mercy endures forever. Amen.

Upon Bringing an Offering to God

We give Thee but Thine own whatever the gift may be. All that we have is Thine alone, a trust O Lord from Thee. Amen.

Prayer at the Beginning of the Day

O Lord, almighty, and everlasting God, You have brought us in safety to this new day; preserve us with Your mighty power, that we may not fall into sin, nor be overcome in adversity; and in all we do, direct us to the fulfilling of Your purpose; through Christ our Lord. Amen.

Prayer at the Close of the Day

Be present, merciful God, and protect us through the hours of this night, so that we who are wearied by the changes and chances of life may find our rest in You; through Jesus Christ our Lord. Amen.

Prayer for God's Peace

O God, from whom came all holy desires, all good counsels, and all just works: Give to us Your servants, that peace which the world cannot give, that our hearts may be set to obey Your commandments; and also that we, being defended from the fear of our enemies, may live in peace and quietness; through Christ our Lord. Amen.

Prayer of Thanksgiving

God our Father: You go before us, drawing us into the future where You are. We thank You for the hope we have in Your word, the good promises of peace, healing, and justice. For signs of Your patience, we are grateful. For every call to duty, we give You praise. Help us, O God, to follow where You lead until the day of our Lord Jesus, when the kingdom will come and You rule the world; for the sake of Christ our Savior. Amen.

– "THE WORSHIP BOOK,"
WESTMINISTER PRESS, PHILADELPHIA, PA 1970, 1972

Prayer of God's Mercy

Almighty and everlasting God, who hatest nothing that Thou hast made, and dost forgive the sins of those who are penitent: Create and make in us new and contrite hearts, that we, truly lamenting our sins and acknowledging our wickedness, may obtain of Thee, the God of all mercy, perfect remission and forgiveness; through Jesus Christ our Lord. Amen.

– "THE METHODIST HYMNAL,"
THE METHODIST PUBLISHING HOUSE, NASHVILLE, TN 1966

Prayer of Courage

O God, who for our redemption didst give Thine only begotten Son to the death on the cross, and by his glorious resurrection hast delivered us from the power of our enemy: Grant us so to die daily to sin that we may evermore live with Him in the joy of His resurrection; through Jesus Christ our Lord. Amen.

– "THE METHODIST HYMNAL"

Another Prayer of Thanksgiving

We give thanks to You, God our Father, for mercy that reaches out, for patience that waits our return-ing, and for Your love that is ever ready to welcome sinners. We praise You that in Jesus Christ You came to us with forgiveness, and that by Your Holy Spirit, You move us to repent and receive Your love. Though we are sinners, You are faithful and worthy of all praise. We praise You, great God, in Jesus Christ our Lord. Amen.

– "THE WORSHIP BOOK"

Prayer for Strength

Grant to us, Lord, we beseech Thee, the spirit to think and do always such things as are right; that we, who cannot do anything that is good without Thee, may by Thee be enabled to live according to Thy will; through Jesus Christ our Lord. Amen.

— "THE METHODIST HYMNAL"

Prayer of Forgiveness

Almighty God, our Heavenly Father, who of Your great mercy has promised forgiveness of sins to all them that with hearty repentance and true faith turn to You, have mercy upon us; pardon and deliver us from all our sins; confirm and strengthen us in all goodness; and bring us to everlasting life, through Jesus Christ our Lord. Amen.

— "THE PRESBYTERIAN BOOK OF COMMON WORSHIP,"
BOARD OF CHRISTIAN EDUCATION OF THE PRESBYTERIAN
CHURCH IN THE UNITED STATES OF AMERICA, PHILADELPHIA,
PA, 1946

Prayer for God's Blessing

Grant, we beseech Thee, almighty God, that the words which we have heard this day with our outward ears may, though Thy grace, be so grafted inwardly in our hearts, that they may bring forth in us the fruit of good living, to the honor and praise of Thy name; through Jesus Christ our Lord. Amen.

— "THE METHODIST HYMNAL"

Prayer for Wisdom

Most holy and merciful God; We acknowledge and confess before You our sinful nature prone to evil and to neglect the good. You alone know how often we have sinned; in wasting Your gifts; in forgetting Your love. But You, O Lord, have mercy upon us; who are ashamed and sorry for all we have done to displease You. Teach us to hate our errors; Cleanse us from our secret faults; and forgive our sins; for the sake of Your Son. And O most holy and loving God; help us to live in Your light and walk in Your ways; according to the commandments of Jesus Christ our Lord. Amen.

– "The Presbyterian Book of Common Worship"

Prayer for Our Home

Almighty God, our Heavenly Father, who sets the solitary in families, we commend to Your continual care the homes in which Your people dwell. But far from them, we beseech You, every root of bitterness, the desire of vainglory, and the pride of life. Fill them with faith, virtue, knowledge, temperance, patience, godliness. Knit together in constant affection those who, in holy wedlock, have been made one. Turn the hearts of the parents to the children, and the hearts of the children to the parents; and so kindle charity among us all, that we may ever have for each other kindly affection and love for all; through Jesus Christ our Lord. Amen.

— "The Presbyterian Book of Common Worship"

Prayer of Thanksgiving

Almighty God, Father of all mercies, we, Your unworthy servants, do give You most humble and hearty thanks for all Your goodness and loving kindness to us, and to all.

We bless You for our creation, preservation, and all the blessings of this life; but above all, for Your inestimable love in the redemption of the world by our Lord Jesus Christ; for the means of grace, and for the hope of glory. And, we beseech You, give us that due sense of all Your mercies, that our hearts may be unfeignedly thankful; and that we show forth Your praise, not only with our lips, but in our lives, by giving up ourselves to Your service, and by walking before You in holiness and righteousness all our days; through Jesus Christ our Lord, to whom, with You and the Holy Spirit, be all honor and glory, world without end. Amen.

— "The Book of Common Prayer,"
Protestant Episcopal Church in USA, 1979

Prayer for the President and Others in Authority

O Lord, our heavenly Father, whose glory is in all the world, and who dost from Thy throne behold all the dwellers upon earth: Most heartily we beseech Thee, with Thy favor to behold and bless Thy servants, the President of the United States, the Governor of this state, and all others who bear rule throughout the world. Grant them wisdom and strength to know and to do Thy will. Fill them with the love of truth and righteousness. So rule their hearts and prosper their endeavors, that law and order, justice and peace may everywhere prevail, to the honor of Thy holy name; through Jesus Christ our Lord. Amen.

— "THE METHODIST HYMNAL"

Prayer for Our Country

Almighty God, who has given us this good land for our heritage; we humbly beseech You that we may always prove ourselves a people mindful of Your favor and glad to do Your will. Bless our land with honorable industry, sound learning, and pure manners. Save us from violence, discord, and confusion; from pride and arrogance, and from every evil way. Defend our liberties, and fashion into one united people the multitudes brought hither out of many kindreds and tongues. Empower with the spirit of wisdom those to whom in Your Name we entrust the authority of government, that there may be justice and peace at home, and that, through obedience to Your law, we may show forth Your praise among the nations of the earth. In the time of prosperity, fill our hearts with thankfulness, and in the day of trouble, suffer not our trust in You to fail; all which we ask through Jesus Christ our Lord. Amen.

– "THE BOOK OF COMMON PRAYER"

Prayer of Trust

Trust in the Lord, and do good; so shalt thou dwell in the land, and verily thou shalt be fed. Delight thyself also in the Lord; and He shall give thee the desires of thine heart.

Commit thy way into the Lord; trust also in Him; and He shall bring it to pass. And He shall bring forth thy righteousness as the light, and thy judgment as the noonday.

– "BAPTIST RESPONSIVE READING"

Prayer Regarding God's Word

All scripture is given by inspiration of God, and is profitable for doctrine, for reproof, for correction, for instruction in righteousness; that the man of God may be perfect, thoroughly furnished unto all good works.

The law of the Lord is perfect, converting the soul; the testimony of the Lord is sure, making wise the simple. The statutes of the Lord are right, rejoicing the heart; the commandment of the Lord is pure, enlightening the eyes.

Thy word is a lamp unto my feet, and a light unto my path. The entrance of Thy words giveth light; it giveth understanding unto the simple. The word of God is quick, and powerful, and sharper than any two-edged sword, piercing even to the dividing asunder of soul and spirit, and of the joints and marrow, and is a discerner of the thoughts and intents of the heart.

– "Baptist Responsive Reading"

Prayer of Faith

God commendeth His love toward us, in that, while we were yet sinners, Christ died for us. Much more then, being now justified by His blood, we shall be saved from wrath through Him. For if, when we were enemies, we were reconciled to God by the death of His Son, much more, being reconciled, we shall be saved by His life. And not only so, but we also find joy in God through our Lord Jesus Christ, by whom we have now received the atonement.

For by grace are ye saved through faith; and that not of yourselves; it is the gift of God; not of words, lest any man should boast.

– "Baptist Responsive Reading"

The Ten Commandments of God

God spoke, and these were His words: "I am the Lord your God who brought you out of Egypt where you were slaves.

"Worship no god but Me.

"Do not make for yourselves images of anything in heaven or on earth or in the water under the earth. Do not bow down to any idol or worship it, because I am the Lord your God and I tolerate no rivals. I bring punishment on those who hate Me and on their descendants down to the third and fourth generation. But I show My love to thousands of generations of those who love Me and obey My laws.

"Do not use My name for evil purposes, for I, the Lord your God, will punish anyone who misuses My name.

"Observe the Sabbath and keep it holy. You have six days in which to do your work, but the seventh day is a day of rest dedicated to Me. On that day no one is to work—neither you, your children, your slaves, your animals, nor the foreigners who live in your country. In six days, I, the Lord, made the earth, the sky, the seas, and everything in them, but on the seventh day I rested. That is why I, the Lord, blessed the Sabbath and made it holy.

"Respect your father and your mother so that you may live a long time in the land that I am giving you.

"Do not commit murder.

"Do not commit adultery.

"Do not steal.

"Do not accuse anyone falsely.

"Do not desire another man's house; do not desire his wife, his slaves, his cattle, his donkeys, or anything else that he owns."

— EXODUS 20:1-17

Youth
Psalms

Garden of the Bible,
Boys Town Campus

Psalm 8
God's Glory and Our Dignity

O Lord, Our Lord,
Your greatness is seen in all the world.
Your praise reaches up to the heavens;
   it is sung by children and babies.
You are safe and secure from all Your enemies;
You stop anyone who opposes You.
When I look at the sky,
which You have made, at the moon and the stars,
which You set in their places –
what is man, that You think of him;
   mere man, that You care for him?
Yet You made him inferior only to Yourself.
You crowned him with glory and honor.
You appointed him ruler over everything
   You made;
You placed him over all creation;
   sheep and cattle, and the wild animals too;
the birds and the fish and the creatures in
   the seas.
O Lord, our Lord, Your greatness is seen in
   all the world!

– ALL PSALMS ARE FROM THE "GOOD NEWS BIBLE."

Psalm 19
The Handwriting in the Heavens

How clearly the sky reveals God's glory!

How plainly it shows what He has done!

Each day announces it to the following day;
  each night repeats it to the next.

No speech or words are used, no sound is heard;

yet their message goes out to all the world

and is heard to the ends of the earth.

God made a home in the sky for the sun;

it comes out in the morning like a happy
  bridegroom,

like an athlete eager to run a race.

It starts at one end of the sky and goes across

to the other. Nothing can hide from its heat.

Psalm 23
The Lord Is My Shepherd

The Lord is my shepherd;
  I have everything I need.

He lets me rest in fields of green grass and
  leads me to quiet pools of fresh water.

He gives me new strength.

He guides me in the right paths,
  as He has promised.

Even if I go through the deepest darkness,
    I will not be afraid, Lord, for You are with me.

Your shepherd's rod and staff protect me.

You prepare a banquet for me, where all my
    enemies can see me;

You welcome me as an honored guest and
    fill my cup to the brim.

I know that Your goodness and love will be with
    me all my life;

and Your house will be my home as long
    as I live.

Psalm 51 (1-4, 6-15)
An Act of Contrition

Be merciful to me, O God, because of Your
    constant love.

Because of Your great mercy wipe away my sins!

Wash away all my evil and make me clean from
    my sin!

I recognize my faults; I am always conscious of my
    sins.

I have sinned against You – only against You –
    and done what You consider evil.

So You are right in judging me; You are justified in
    condemning me.

Sincerity and truth are what You require;
    fill my mind with Your wisdom.

Remove my sin, and I will be clean;
   wash me, and I will be whiter than snow.

Let me hear the sounds of joy and gladness;
   and though You have crushed me and
   broken me, I will be happy once again.

Close Your eyes to my sins and wipe out
   all my evil.

Create a pure heart in me, O God, and
   put a new and loyal spirit in me.

Do not banish me from Your presence;
   do not take Your holy spirit away from me.

Give me again the joy that comes from Your
   salvation, and make me willing to obey You.

Then I will teach sinners Your commands, and
   they will turn back to You.

Spare my life, O God, and save me and
   I will gladly proclaim Your righteousness.

Help me to speak, Lord, and I will praise You.

Psalm 100
A Hymn of Praise

Sing to the Lord, all the world!

Worship the Lord with joy; come before
   Him with happy songs!

Acknowledge that the Lord is God.

He made us, and we belong to Him;
   we are His people, we are His flock.

Enter the Temple gates with thanksgiving;
   go into its courts with praise.

Give thanks to Him and praise Him.

The Lord is good; His love is eternal and
   His faithfulness lasts forever.

Psalm 139
God's Care and Love

Lord, You have examined me and You know me.

You know everything I do; from far away
   You understand all my thoughts.

You see me, whether I am working or resting; You
   know all my actions.

Even before I speak, You already know what
   I will say.

You are all around me on every side;
   You protect me with Your power.

Your knowledge of me is too deep;
   it is beyond my understanding.

Where could I go to escape from You?

Where could I get away from Your presence?

If I went up to heaven, You would be there;
   if I lay down in the world of the dead,
   You would be there.

If I flew away beyond the east or lived
   in the farthest place in the west,
   You would be there to help me.

I could ask the darkness to hide me or the light
    around me to turn into night, but even darkness
    is not dark for You,
    and the night is as bright as the day.
Darkness and light are the same to You.
You created every part of me; You put me
    together in my mother's womb,
    I praise You because You are to be feared;
All You do is strange and wonderful.
    I know it with all my heart.
When my bones were being formed, carefully
    put together in my mother's womb, when
    I was growing there in secret, You knew that I
    was there—You saw me before I was born.
The days allotted to me had all been recorded in
    Your book, before many of them ever began.
O God, how difficult I find Your thoughts;
    how many of them there are?
If I counted them, they would be more
    than the grains of sand.
When I awake, I am still with You.
O God, how I wish You would kill the wicked!
How I wish violent men would leave me alone!
They say wicked things about You;
    they speak evil things against Your name.
O Lord, how I hate those who hate You!
How I despise those who rebel against You!
I hate them with a total hatred;
    I regard them as my enemies.

Examine me, O God, and know my mind;
   test me, and discover my thoughts.
Find out if there is any evil in me and guide me in
   the everlasting way.

Psalm 145
God's Grandeur and Goodness

I will proclaim Your greatness,
   my God and king;
I will thank You for ever and ever.
Everyday I will thank You;
   I will praise You forever and ever.
The Lord is great and is to be highly praised;
   His greatness is beyond understanding.
What You have done will be praised from one
   generation to the next; they will proclaim
   Your mighty acts.
They will speak of Your glory and majesty,
and I will meditate on Your wonderful deeds.
People will speak of Your mighty deeds,
   and I will proclaim Your greatness, and
   sing about Your kindness.
The Lord is loving and merciful, slow to become
   angry and full of constant love.
He is good to everyone and has compassion on all
   He made.

All Your creatures, Lord, will praise You,
and all Your people will give You thanks.

They will speak of the glory of Your royal power
and tell of Your might, so that everyone will
know Your mighty deeds and the glorious
majesty of Your kingdom.

Your rule is eternal, and You are king forever.

Hymn-Poems to Pray in the Quiet of One's Room

Father Flanagan and Boys Town Choir, 1945

Tell Me the Old, Old Story

Tell me the Old, Old Story, of unseen things
above,
Of Jesus and His glory, of Jesus and His love;
Tell me the story simply, as to a little child,
For I am weak and weary and helpless and
defiled.
Tell me the Old, Old Story, tell me the Old,
Old Story,
Tell me the Old, Old, Story of Jesus and
His love.

Tell me the story, slowly, that I may take it in,
That wonderful redemption, God's remedy
for sin;
Tell me the story often, for I forgot so soon,
The "early dew" of morning has passed
away at noon.
Tell me the Old, Old Story, tell me the Old,
Old Story,
Tell me the Old, Old, Story of Jesus and
His love.

Tell me the story softly, with earnest tones
and grave;
Remember I'm the sinner whom Jesus came
to save;
Tell me the story always, if you would really be,
In any time of trouble, a comforter to me.

Tell me the Old, Old Story, tell me the Old,
Old Story,
Tell me the Old, Old, Story of Jesus and
His love.

Tell me the same old story, when you have
a cause to fear
That this world's empty glory is costing me
too dear;
Yes, and when that world's glory is dawning
on my soul,
Tell me the Old, Old Story: "Christ Jesus makes
thee whole."
Tell me the Old, Old Story, tell me the Old,
Old Story,
Tell me the Old, Old, Story of Jesus and
His love.

Softly and Tenderly

Softly and tenderly Jesus is calling,
Calling for you and for me;
See, on the portals He's waiting and watching,
Watching for you and for me.
Come home, come home,
Ye who are weary, come home;
Earnestly, tenderly, Jesus is calling,
Calling, O sinner, come home!

Why should we tarry when Jesus is pleading,
Pleading for you and for me?
Why should we linger and heed not His mercies,
Mercies for you and for me?
Come home, come home,
Ye who are weary, come home;
Earnestly, tenderly, Jesus is calling,
Calling, O sinner, come home!

Time is now fleeting, the moments are passing,
Passing from you and from me;
Shadows are gathering, death's night is coming,
Coming for you and for me.
Come home, come home,
Ye who are weary, come home;
Earnestly, tenderly, Jesus is calling,
Calling, O sinner, come home!

O for the wonderful love He has promised,
Promised for you and for me!
Though we have sinned, He has mercy and pardon,
Pardon for you and for me.
Come home, come home,
Ye who are weary, come home;
Earnestly, tenderly, Jesus is calling,
Calling, O sinner, come home!

What a Friend
We Have in Jesus

What a friend we have in Jesus,
All our sins and griefs to bear!
What a privilege to carry
Everything to God in prayer!
O what peace we often forfeit,
O what needless pain we bear,
All because we do not carry
Everything to God in prayer!

Have we trials and temptations?
Is there trouble anywhere?
We should never be discouraged,
Take it to the Lord in prayer.
Can we find a friend so faithful
Who will all our sorrows share?
Jesus knows our every weakness,
Take it to the Lord in prayer.

Are we weak and heavy laden,
Cumbered with a load of care?
Precious Savior, still our refuge
Take it to the Lord in prayer.
Do thy friends despise, forsake thee?
Take it to the Lord in prayer;
In His arms He'll take and shield thee,
Thou wilt find a solace there.

A Mighty Fortress

A mighty fortress is our God
A bulwark never failing
Our helper He amid the flood
Of mortal ills prevailing;
For still our ancient Foe
Doth seek to work us woe;
His craft and power are great,
And armed with cruel hate,
On earth is not his equal.
Did we in our own strength confide,
Our striving would be losing;
Were not the right man on our side,
The man of God's own choosing;
Dost ask who that may be?
Christ Jesus, it is He;
Lord Sabbath His name,
From age to age to the same,
And He must win the battle.
And though this world, with devils filled,
Should threaten to undo us;
We will not fear, for God hath willed
His truth to triumph through us;
The Prince of Darkness grim,
We tremble not for him;
His rage we can endure,
For Lo! his doom is sure,
One little word shall fell him.
That word above all earthly powers.
The Spirit and the gifts are ours
Through Him who with us sideth;

Let goods and kindred go,
This mortal life also;
The body they may kill:
God's truth abideth still;
His kingdom is forever. Amen.

Amazing Grace

Amazing grace! How sweet the sound,
that saved a wretch like me!
I once was lost but now am found,
was blind, but now I see.

Through many dangers, toils and snares,
I have already come;
'Tis grace hath brought me safe thus far,
and grace will lead me home.

When we've been there ten thousand years,
been shining as the sun;
We've no less days to sing God's praise
than when we first begun.

Holy God, We Praise Thy Name

Holy God, we praise Thy Name,
Lord of all, we bow before Thee;
All on earth Thy scepter claim,
All in Heaven above adore Thee,
Infinite Thy vast domain,

Everlasting is Thy reign.
Hark the loud celestial hymn,
Angel choirs above are raising!
Cherubim and Seraphim
In unceasing chorus praising;
Fill Thy Heavens with sweet accord;
Holy holy holy Lord!
Holy Father, Holy Son,
Holy Spirit, Three we name Thee,
While in essence only One,
Undivided God we claim Thee!
And adoring bend the knee,
While we own the mystery.

America, the Beautiful

O beautiful for spacious skies,
For amber waves of grain,
For purple mountain majesties
Above the fruited plain!
America! America!
God shed His grace on thee,
And crown thy good with brotherhood
From sea to shining sea.

O beautiful for pilgrim feet,
Whose stern, impassioned stress,
A thoroughfare for freedom beat
Across the wilderness!

America! America!
God mend thine ev'ry flaw,
Confirm thy soul in self-control,
Thy liberty in law.

Come, Holy Ghost

Come, Holy Ghost, Creator blest,
And in our heart take up Thy rest;
Come with Thy grace and heav'nly aid
To fill the hearts which Thou hast made,
To fill the hearts which Thou has made.

O Comforter, to Thee we cry,
Thou heav'nly gift of God most high,
Thou font of life and fire of love,
And sweet anointing from above.
And sweet anointing from above.
Praise be to thee, Father and Son,
And Holy Spirit, with them one;
And may the Son on us bestow
The gifts that from the Spirit flow.
The gifts that from the Spirit flow.

O Come, O Come, Emmanuel

O come, O come, Emmanuel,
And ransom captive Israel,
That mourns in lonely exile here
Until the Son of God appear.
Rejoice! Rejoice!

Emmanuel shall come to thee, O Israel.
O come, thou day-spring, come and cheer
Our spirits by thine advent here;
Disperse the gloomy clouds of night
And death's dark shadow put to fight.
O come, desire of nations, bind
In one the hearts of humankind;
Bid ev'ry sad division cease
And be thyself our Prince of Peace.

Lo, How A Rose E'er Blooming

Lo, how a rose e'er blooming,
From tender root has grown;
From Jesse's offspring coming
To all the world made known.
It came amid the cold,
A bright and shining blossom
As prophets had foretold.
The sweet rose of this story
Isaiah did proclaim.
What God ordained for glory,
By blessed Mary came.
The Child the Virgin bore,
The world's salvation bringing
Through him for evermore.

Sing of Mary

Sing of Mary, pure and lowly,
Virgin mother undefiled,
Sing of God's own Son most holy,
Who became her little child.
Fairest child of fairest mother,
God the Lord who came to earth,
Word made flesh, our very brother,
Takes our nature by His birth.
Sing of Jesus, son of Mary,
In the home at Nazareth.
Toil and labor cannot weary
Love enduring unto death.
Constant was the love He gave her,
Though He went forth from her side,
Forth to preach, and heal and suffer,
Till on Calvary He died.
Glory be to God the Father;
Glory be to God the Son;
Glory be to God the Spirit;
Glory to the Three in One.
From the heart of blessed Mary,
From all saints the song ascends,
And the Church the strain re-echoes
Unto earth's remotest ends.

What Child Is This

What child is this, who laid to rest,
On Mary's lap is sleeping?
Whom angels greet with anthems sweet,
While shepherds watch are keeping?
This, this is Christ the King,
Whom shepherds guard and angels sing;
Haste, haste, to bring Him laud,
The Babe, the Son of Mary.
Why lies He in such mean estate,
Where ox and ass are feeding?
Good Christian, fear for sinners here
The silent Word is pleading.
Nails, spears shall pierce Him through,
The cross be borne for me, for you;
Hail, hail, the Word made flesh,
The Babe, the Son of Mary!
So bring Him incense, gold and myrrh,
Come, peasant, king, to own Him;
The King of kings salvation brings,
Let loving hearts enthrone Him.
Raise, raise the songs on high,
The Virgin sings her lullaby:
Joy, joy, for Christ is born,
The Babe, the Son of Mary!

Were You There

Were you there when they crucified my Lord?
Were you there when they crucified my Lord?
Oh! Sometimes it causes me to tremble,
   tremble, tremble,
Were you there when they crucified my Lord?

Were you there when they nailed Him to
   the tree?
Were you there when they nailed Him to
   the tree?
Oh! Sometimes it causes me to tremble,
   tremble, tremble,
Were you there when they nailed Him to
   the tree?

Were you there when they laid Him in the tomb?
Were you there when they laid Him in the tomb?
Oh! Sometimes it causes me to tremble,
   tremble, tremble,
Were you there when they laid Him in the tomb?

I Know That My Redeemer Lives

I know that my Redeemer lives;
What joy the blest assurance gives!
He lives, He lives, who once was dead;
He lives, my everlasting Head!
He lives, to bless me with His love;
He lives to plead for me above;

He lives, my hungry soul to feed;
He lives, to help in time of need.

He lives, and grants me daily breath;
He lives, and I shall conquer death;
He lives, my mansion to prepare;
He lives, to bring me safely there.
He lives, all glory to His name;
He lives, my Savior, still the same;
What joy the blest assurance gives;
I know that my Redeemer lives! Amen

Jesus Christ Is Risen Today

Jesus Christ is risen today, Alleluia!
Our triumphant holy day, Alleluia!
Who did once, upon the cross, Alleluia!
Suffer to redeem our loss, Alleluia!

Hymns of praise then let us sing, Alleluia!
Unto Christ, our heavenly King, Alleluia!
Who endured the cross and grave, Alleluia!
Sinners to redeem and save, Alleluia!

Sing we to our God above, Alleluia!
Praise eternal as His love; Alleluia!
Praise Him, all ye heavenly host, Alleluia!
Father, Son, and Holy Ghost, Alleluia! Amen.

The Strife Is O'er, the Battle Done

The strife is o'er, the battle done;
The victory of life is won;
The song of triumph has begun;
Alleluia!

The powers of death have done their worst,
But Christ their legions hath dispersed;
Let shouts of holy joy outburst;
Alleluia!

The three sad days have quickly sped;
He rises glorious from the dead;
All glory to our risen Head!
Alleluia!

Lord, by the stripes which wounded Thee,
From death's dread sting Thy servants free,
That we may live and sing to Thee;
Alleluia!

O Sons and Daughters, Let Us Sing

O sons and daughters, let us sing!
The King of heaven, the glorious King,
O'er death today rose triumphing,
Alleluia! Alleluia!

That Easter morn at break of day,
The faithful women went their way

To seek the tomb where Jesus lay,
Alleluia! Alleluia!

An angel clad in white they see,
Who sat and spake unto the three,
"Your Lord doth go to Galilee,"
Alleluia! Alleluia!

How blest are they who have not seen,
And yet whose faith hath constant been;
For they eternal life shall win,
Alleluia! Alleluia!

On this most holy day of days,
Our hearts and voices, Lord,
We raise to Thee, in jubilee and praise,
Alleluia! Alleluia!

A Final
Word

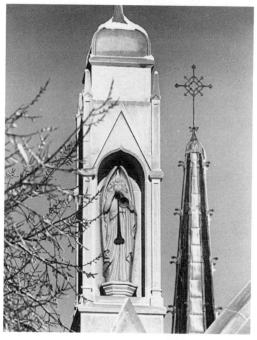

Angel on Chambers Chapel,
Boys Town Campus

More Prayers and Help in the Bible

When you feel unloved	Romans 8:35-39
When in need	John 14
When you have sinned	Psalm 51
When you are worried	Matthew 6:19-34
If you have the blues	Psalm 34
When God seems far away	Psalm 139
If you are discouraged	Isaiah 40
If you are lonely or fearful	Psalm 23
If you feel down and out	Romans 8:39
When you want courage	Joshua 1
If you get bitter or critical	I Corinthians 13
For a great invitation	Isaiah 55
When discouraged	Psalm 37

When things seem to go from bad to worse
II Tim. 3; Heb. 13

When friends seem to go back on you
Matthew 5; I Corinthians 13

When sorrow overtakes you	Psalm 46
When tempted to do wrong	Matthew 4
When you can't fall asleep	Psalm 4
When you have quarreled	Matthew 18; Eph. 4
When worries oppress you	Matthew 6
If you are facing a crisis	Isaiah 55
If you are jealous	James 3
If you are bored	I John 3
When everything is well	James 2:1-17

When you are in a position of responsibility

11 Cor. 8:1-15

When you think God seems far away   Luke 10

When you are lonely or fearful   Luke 8
or I Peter 4

When you have sinned   Psalm 51
or I John 1

When you want a worshipful mood   John 4:1-5

When you are concerned with God in
national life   Isaiah 41:8-20

If you bear a grudge   Luke 6

If you have been disobedient   Luke 5

If you need forgiveness   Phileman

If you are sick or in pain   Isaiah 26

To find the Ten Commandments   Deut. 5

To find the Shepherd Psalm   Psalm 23

To find the Birth of Jesus   Luke 2

To find the Beatitudes   Matthew 5:1-12

To find the Sermon on the Mount

Matthew 5, 6, 7

To find the Lord's Prayer   Luke 11:1-13

To find the Great Commandments

Matthew 22:34-40

To find the parable of the Good Samaritan

Luke 10

To find the parable of the Prodigal Son   Luke 15

To find the parable of the Sower   Luke 8

To find the Crucifixion, Death and Resurrection
of Jesus   Matthew 26, 27, 28